Meeting the
Big-Box Challenge:

Planning, Design, and Regulatory Strategies

JENNIFER EVANS–COWLEY, AICP

TABLE OF CONTENTS

Meeting the
Big-Box Challenge:

Planning, Design, and Regulatory Strategies

f the rapid expansion of the world's leading retailer, Wal-Mart, is any indication, the large-scale retail format known as "big-box" will have a growing impact on communities across the U.S. and around the globe. Consider: In 2004, 82 percent of United States households made a purchase at a Wal-Mart store (CNBC 2005). Wal-Mart is the nation's largest employer (1.2 million workers), seller of retail goods ($280 billion annually), and owner of corporate real estate (911 million square feet) (Boarnet et al. 2005, 433).

These statistics and others say two things: consumers are increasingly shopping at Wal-Mart and other big-box retailers (as we will refer to them in this report), and big-box stores in all their variety and types and owners are in nearly every community. *The Hometown Advantage* (www. newrules.org), for example, in a November 16, 2005, story reports that a leaked memo from Wal-Mart shows plans for 484 new or expanded stores in the United States in 2006, which is 100 more than the company had previously reported, totaling an additional 90 million square feet of development. And in April 2005, Wal-Mart announced it would donate enough land on an acre-for-acre basis to the National Fish and Wildlife Foundation to offset the additional 138,000 acres it intends to develop in the U.S. over the next 10 years.

Big-box retailers, despite growing opposition to some of them on a variety of grounds (aesthetic, destruction of local business, wage levels), are here to stay and will continue to command a greater presence in the retail sector for a number of reasons.

Big-box retailers, despite growing opposition to some of them on a variety of grounds (aesthetic, destruction of local business, wage levels), are here to stay and will continue to command a greater presence in the retail sector for a number of reasons. Wal-Mart's corporate strategy of "vertical integration" (the process in which several steps in the production and/or distribution of a product or service are controlled by a single company or entity in order to increase that company's or entity's power in the marketplace), economy of scale, and other cost-saving measures have earned the admiration of business school professors and Wall Street watchers alike. To survive, competing retailers must either achieve similar levels of productivity or differentiate their goods and services from those offered by Wal-Mart. There is evidence that the big-box is the future retail model. Consider this from "The Revolution in Retail Trade" by J. Michael Reidy and Robert H. McGuckin (2005):

> Better information about sales and inventories has spawned faster, more efficient order and delivery systems. Orders with suppliers, once large and infrequent, have diminished in size and increased in frequency, creating incentives and advantages for larger, "big box" stores.

Critics of the Wal-Mart approach contend that these cost-cutting pressures drive a "race to the bottom" among retail employers, with decreased wages, higher levels of public assistance required to support retail workers, and other social costs attributable to corporate practices—all of which will be discussed in this PAS Report. The battle over unionized grocery worker wages in southern California after the introduction of Wal-Mart supercenters reinforced these critics' concerns and triggered regulatory responses across the state (Boarnet et al. 2005).

There is increasing pressure on big-box retailers to generate greater returns for their stockholders, forcing them to consider expansion into areas where they have had no or little presence. Wal-Mart has hired top campaign managers to proactively combat anti-Wal-Mart messages and improve its image in consumers' minds to pave the way for such expansion (Barbaro 2005). This quote from Wal-Mart's Chief Executive Officer, Lee Scott, sheds light on the company's attitude to community opposition:

> [W]hen you have a group of people, a small group of people who don't want you in the community, does that mean you are not going to go there? I mean I don't think we'd have a store. You would simply have everybody who is those people who don't care for us going to each community saying we now have five people, 100 people, 150 people who don't want a Wal-Mart.... Go back and look at the record of the places where we had difficulty getting in and look at how busy the stores are on a Saturday. Is it the customers that didn't want us or is it a particular group? (CNBC 2005)

Facing more rigorous regulation in response to big-box stores and their practices, Wal-Mart and other big-box retailers have not been reluctant to go to the ballot box to get what they want, as is evidenced by efforts in places as diverse as Inglewood, California, and Monroe, Wisconsin (these efforts can be monitored at a number of sites, including www.newrules.org; www.walmartwatch.com; www.sprawl-busters.com; and www.wakeupwalmart.com). Opponents of big-box retail have turned to the ballot box as well, and their successes and failures can be monitored at the same websites.

To avoid taking decisions out of the hands of professional planners through the ballot box or litigation, planners need to be able to meet the challenges posed by big-box retailers and to make their presence a positive rather than a negative influence on the community. There are such opportunities, especially in urban areas. For instance, retailers, finding that the suburban retail markets are saturating, are increasingly considering urban locations as emerging markets. This opens up opportunities for adaptive reuse of industrial buildings into chain stores, making historic preservation planners happy, and increases the viability of the inner city as a retail location, helping urban economic development planners trying to bring back goods and services to distressed communities. (See the section below on multistory big-box stores for illustrations and examples.)

This report will provide citizens, planners, and officials with a number of planning, design, and regulatory techniques that have been used in communities and by the companies themselves in meeting the demands and desires of both citizens and retailers.

While this report considers the traditional issues associated with big-box retail establishments (particularly aesthetics and their impact on the existing local retail sector), it also looks at the salaries and job benefits (or lack of them) of employees at big-box retailers, a subject that continues drawing scrutiny (for example, a national conference on the subject took place on November 4, 2005, while this report was being edited).

Retailers have shown they can be responsive to aesthetic concerns. But the jury is still out on the wage and benefits issues. This controversy about wages and benefits is a subject about which planners need to be better informed and for which they need tools beyond land-use regulations. Specifically, they will need to supplement land-use controls with an economic impact assessment to ensure that each community independently weighs the benefits and costs of hosting big-box retail establishments.

The findings reported here are primarily based on a survey conducted by the author and the American Planning Association's Planning Advisory Service of more than 600 planners. A total of 217 planners from across the country responded to the survey (a response rate of 36 percent). Results of this survey inform the suggestions and conclusions of this report.

This report has five major sections:

1. **"What is a big-box retail store?"** describes the types of big-box retailers and provides definitions from zoning ordinances.

2. **" Planning issues created by the big-box and its business practices"** describes the two categories of planning issues. The first are "traditional" planning problems: aesthetics and traffic generation. The second category concerns economic development. What positive and negative effects do big-box retail establishments have on the local economy? We will outline these issues here and suggest ways in which planners can respond to them.

3. **"Regulatory approaches"** shows how communities have responded or anticipated the impact of big-box stores, including regulations that limit store size and some that control design.

4. **"What to Do When the Big-box Closes: "White Elephant" Ordinances, and Adaptive Reuse"** highlights examples of how communities have responded to the problem of empty big-box retail stores.

To avoid taking decisions out of the hands of professional planners through the ballot box or litigation, planners need to be able to meet the challenges posed by big-box retailers and to make their presence a positive rather than a negative influence on the community.

Figures 1-4. *The all-too-typical big-box store. Garish, vast parking lots in front of the store—just a characterless box.*

All photos by Corrin Hoegen

Figures 5-9. Attempts to upgrade the appearance of big-box retail establishments (e.g., a willingness to forgo standard corporate signage colors; variations in the façade colors; varied setbacks; some native landscaping; and parapets to screen mechanical equipment on the roof) have resulted in minor improvements, but the general formula seems to persist.

5. **"Recommendations and suggestions"** summarizes the major approaches communities are using and offers suggestions as to how communities can best plan to respond to the many challenges of big-box retail.

WHAT IS A BIG-BOX RETAIL STORE?

In the survey, when asked how they define big-box retail, planners' answers varied widely. Definitions are important because they form the "threshold" for regulations. The following description combines their responses to form a more generic description and definition of the big-box retail store.

A big-box retail store is typically a one-story warehouse building with a height of 30 feet or more, simple and rectangular in construction, made of corrugated metal, concrete block, or brick-faced walls, and ranging in size from 20,000 to 260,000 square feet. It is generally a stand-alone building with a large parking lot or part of a larger shopping center. In describing the "function" of a big-box retailer, planners said they delivered inexpensive goods.

Figure 10. How big exactly is a big-box? This graphic from the New Rules Project provides a simple comparison with other retail stores at a glance.

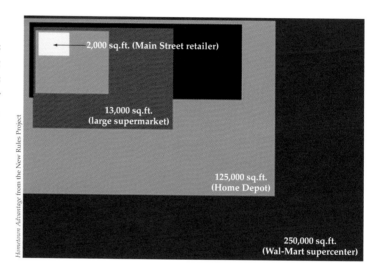

Types of Big-Box Retailers

There are four major types of big-box stores: 1) large general merchandise stores, 2) specialized product, 3) outlet stores, and 5) warehouse clubs. See Table 1 for a compilation of statistics about these types of stores taken from retailers' annual reports and web sites.

Large general merchandise stores. Large general merchandise stores range in size from 30,000 to 260,000 square feet. They offer a wide selection of merchandise at discount prices. Examples of large general merchandise stores include Wal-Mart, Target, and K-Mart. A supercenter is a large general merchandise store with a grocery store inside it (see more about supercenters below).

Figure 11. This Wal-Mart store in Brighton, Colorado, is the quintessential large general merchandise store.

Specialized Product: Specialized product stores (also known as "category killers" because they can dominate smaller competitors who also feature one main product) range in size from 20,000 to 120,000 square feet. They offer a large selection and low prices, but only offer products of one type. Examples of specialized product stores include Barnes and Noble, Best Buy, Staples, and Home Depot.

Outlet Stores: Outlet stores range in size from 20,000 to 180,000 square feet. They are typically outlets for department stores and manufacturers. Examples of outlet stores include Burlington Coat Factory, Big Lots, and Nordstrom Rack.

Warehouse Clubs: Warehouse clubs range in size from 70,000 to 160,000 square feet. They offer a limited selection of goods in bulk at a discounted price, but require a membership to get the discount. Examples of warehouse clubs include Costco and Sam's Club.

Defining the Big Box

It is clear that cities have found a variety of ways to define "big-box retail establishments." We have provided definitions from both the survey and PAS Report No. 521/522, *A Planners Dictionary*. Please note: Although grocery stores may be similar in size to typical big-boxes, ranging from 20,000 to 100,000 square feet, most definitions of big-box retail specifically exempt stores whose primary function is the sale of grocery items.

A definition is important inasmuch as you must be able to define something before you can regulate it. The matter of "capping" the size of an individual retail establishment (namely, no store larger than *x* number of square feet is allowed) may be employed as a means of regulation.

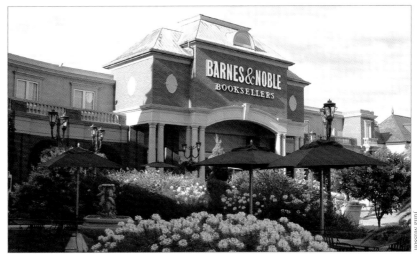

Figure 12. *Barnes and Noble, the bookseller, is a specialized product store. This attractive example is in Woodmere, Ohio.*

Figure 13. *This Big Lots outlet is part of a larger shopping center in California.*

Figure 14. *Costco is a warehouse club.*

TABLE 1. TYPES OF RETAIL BIG-BOX STORES AND AVERAGE SIZE

Type	Website Address	Number of Stores in the United States (at Year End 2004)	Average Size (in square feet) feet)	Size Range	Number of New Stores Planned for 2005
GENERAL MERCHANDISE	www.kmart.com	1,422	95,000	40,000 to 194,000	n/a
	www.kmart.com	58	n/a	Up to 194,000	n/a
	www.meijer.com	170	207,000	n/a	9
	www.target.com	141	n/a	n/a	17
	www.target.com	1,189	126,153	n/a	65
	www.walmartrealty.com	1,353	100,000	30,000–220,000	n/a
	www.walmartrealty.com	1,713	187,000	100,000–261,000	n/a
GROCERY	www.kroger.com	2,532	55,687	n/a	Approximately 40
	www.walmartrealty.com	85	43,000	38,000–55,000	n/a
	www.wholefoods.com	168	49,000	40,000–60,000	10
OUTLET	www.biglots.com	1,502	28,600	10,000–50,000	50 to 70
	www.burlingtoncoatfactory.com	349	78,000	20,000–178,000	12
SPECIALIZED PRODUCT	www.baresandnoble.com	820	27,000	10,000–60,000	30–35
	www.bedbathand beyond.com	660	n/a	20,000–80,000	Historically opened 85 per year in 03 and 04
	www.bordersgifts.com	504	25,100	n/a	15-20
	www.circuitcity.com	617	n/a	n/a	31
	www.homedepot.com	1,890	106,000 plus 22,000 garden area	n/a	n/a
	www.kohls.com	637	77,238	n/a	95
	www.lnt.com	440	n/a	25,000–50,000	45–50
	www.lowes.com	1,087	116,000 plus 31,000 garen area	94,000–116,000 plus 26,000–31,000 garden area	n/a
	www.officedepot.com	969	26,000	n/a	100
	www.petsmart.com	726	n/a	19,000–27,000	100
	www.staples.com	1,426	n/a	n/a	95
	www.toysrus.com/about	1,123	46,000	n/a	59
WAREHOUSE CLUB	www.costco.com	417	136,828	70,000–160,000	30
	www.samsclub.com	551	128,000	70,000–160,000	n/a

General definitions. Municipalities define large merchandise and specialty product big-box retail across a range from 10,000 to more than 200,000 square feet of gross leasable area. Although different names might be used (e.g., "retail sales establishment, bulk"; "retail sales establishment, large"), these definitions all fit the concept of a big-box store. A sampling of typical definitions is as follows:

> A single retail establishment with a building with a gross floor area not less than 25,000 square feet, and which may include fast-food restaurants and other accessory retail uses with an entrance inside the primary retail establishment. (Queen Creek, Arizona)

> A singular retail or wholesale user who occupies no less than 75,000 square feet of gross floor area, typically requires high parking to building area ratios, and has a regional sales market. Regional retail/wholesale sales can include but are not limited to membership warehouse clubs that emphasize bulk sales, discount stores, and department stores. (Redmond, Washington)

> A large-scale (minimum of roughly 100,000 square feet) self-service retail store selling food, drugs, household merchandise, clothing, and a variety of other retail goods. The store may, in some cases, include limited medical services, such as a dentist's office. (Peoria, Illinois)

> A retail structure or group of structures [having] a total in excess of 25,000 square feet of gross floor area. (Concord, North Carolina)

> A retail establishment engaged in selling goods or merchandise to the general public as well as to other retailers, contractors, or businesses, and rendering services incidental to the sale of such goods. Bulk retail involves a high volume of sales of related and/or unrelated products in a warehouse setting and may include membership warehouse clubs, i.e., "big-box" retail. Bulk retail is differentiated from general retail by any of the following characteristics: (1) Items for sale include large, categorized products, e.g., lumber, appliances, household furnishings, electrical and heating fixtures and supplies, wholesale and retail nursery stock, etc.; and may also include a variety of carry out goods, e.g., groceries, household, and personal care products; (2) A large inventory of goods and merchandise is stored on the subject site in high-ceiling warehouse areas, high-rack displays, and/or outdoor storage areas; and (3) High-volume truck traffic, regular pick up and delivery of large items, a designated contractor pick-up area, and high parking-to-building ratios. (Federal Way, Washington)

> A retail establishment, or any combination of retail establishments in a single building, or a movie theater or an indoor recreational use, occupying more than 25,000 square feet of gross floor area, except that no supermarket shall be deemed to be a large retail establishment. (Loveland, Colorado)

> A retail use or any combination of retail uses in a single building, occupying more than 40,000 square feet of Gross Floor Area. (Greeley, Colorado)

> New construction equal to or exceeding 75,000 gross square feet of single plate ground floor and serving a single tenant as a stand-alone retail structure, or as part of a multi-tenant shopping center, or a single plate ground-floor structure serving multi-tenants equal to or exceeding 150,000 gross square feet. (Winston-Salem, North Carolina)

> Any business or businesses that involve, in whole or in part, retail and/or wholesale sales, allowed in the applicable zoning district that:

> 1. share check stands or storage areas,

> 2. share management, or

> 3. are owned, leased, possessed or otherwise controlled, in any manner, directly or indirectly,

> > i. by the same individual(s) or entity(ies), including but not limited to corporation(s), partnership(s), limited liability company(ies) or trust(s), or

ii. by different individuals or entities, including but not limited to corporations, partnerships, limited liability companies or trusts where

    a) such individual(s) or entity(ies) have a controlling ownership or contractual right with the other individual(s) or entity(ies), or

    b) the same individual(s) or entity(ies) act in any manner as an employee, owner, partner, agent, stockholder, director, member, officer or trustee of the entity(ies), and are located within one or more separate buildings or structures within 800 feet of one another, regardless whether they are attached or detached. (Hailey, Idaho)

These definitions are not perfect by any means. Redmond's definition, for example, is unclear. For a retail developer, how would it judge what is a high parking to building area ratio? This definition should state a parking ratio of greater than 1 parking space per 200 square feet, or whatever Redmond views as a high parking to building ratio. Additionally, how is a regional sales market defined? Is this simply a radius of five square miles or something different? The regional sales clause should be removed from this definition. The use of terms like "roughly" in definitions (or, for that matter, regulations) should be avoided.

The final two definitions recognize that big boxes can be smaller than a 100,000-square-foot stand-alone store, which is a good way to deal with that possibility.

Warehouse clubs. Warehouse clubs differ from large general merchandise and specialty product retailers. The stores usually require that customers become members of the club and pay an annual fee in order to continue their membership. Their offerings are typically more limited than those of a general merchandise retailer. See the definition below that employs "stock keeping units" (SKUs) for another example of how warehouse clubs might be distinguished from the general big-box retailer.

> A retail/wholesale hybrid with a varied selection and limited variety of products presented in a warehouse type environment where shoppers are required to pay a membership fee. (Turlock, California; definitions are based on descriptions offered in the Institute of Transportation Engineers *Trip Generation*)

> A retail facility having in excess of 80,000 square feet and not more than 130,000 square feet of floor area which offers for sale a wide variety but limited selection of consumer products; including but not limited to office supplies and equipment, consumer appliances, electronic equipment, furniture, housewares and home furnishings, tools, hardware, recreational and leisure products, automotive equipment and supplies, food and apparel. Distinguishing features of such a facility are that food, beverages, health and beauty products and other products are primarily sold in bulk quantities larger than normally offered by conventional retailers and a restricted selection of other goods and products are offered. The sale of soft goods shall be limited to 20 percent of the floor area of the store, of which not more than 50 percent of said soft goods area shall offer apparel for sale. Not less than 25 percent of the floor area of such facility shall be utilized for the sale of food and beverages. (Stamford, Connecticut)

This definition uses the term "soft goods," which will need to be defined elsewhere in the ordinance.

An exclusive definition for a supercenter/superstore. Supercenters or superstores are the fastest-growing type of retail establishment in the United States since 1998 (Barry 2003), and their growth in numbers has led many communities to establish a separate definition for them. The "nontaxable" provision mentioned in the definitions here is an attempt to limit the impact of these supercenters on local grocery stores (food is nontaxable in California, which is the home of the communities who use this provision). For places where food is taxable, these definitions clearly would not work. This is a perfect example of definitions crafted to deal with specific local issues concerning the presence and operation of big-box retailers.

> A Major Development Project that sells from the premises goods and merchandise, primarily for personal or household use, and whose total Sales Floor Area exceeds 100,000 square feet and that devotes more than 10 percent of sales floor area to the sale of Non-Taxable Merchandise. This definition excludes wholesale clubs or other establishments selling primarily bulk merchandise and charging membership dues or otherwise restricting merchandise sales to customers paying a periodic assessment fee. This definition also excludes the sale or rental of motor vehicles, except for parts and accessories, and the sale of materials used in construction of buildings or other structures, except for paint, fixtures, and hardware. (Los Angeles, California)

> The retail sale from the premises of goods and merchandise, primarily for personal or household use, from stores whose total sales floor area exceeds 100,000 square feet, and which devote more than 10 percent of sales floor area to the sale of non-taxable merchandise, but exclude charging membership dues or otherwise restricting merchandise sales to customers paying a periodic access fee. This classification excludes the sale or rental of motor vehicles, except for parts and accessories, and the sale of materials used in construction of buildings or other structures, except for paint, fixtures, and hardware. (Oakland, California)

> Any single-use building, whether stand alone or within a multi-building development, wherein said single-use building occupies at least 150,000 square feet of building coverage primarily devoted to, or intended for, the sale or display of goods and merchandise for consumption by the general public, including any outdoor sales and display area(s) and storage/stockroom area(s) but excluding any outdoor area for sale of cars, trucks, boats, recreational vehicles, or manufactured dwellings. For the purposes of this definition, calculation of such building coverage shall include all other indoor and outdoor sales areas or customer service area(s) that may be incidental to, but nevertheless share customer walking aisles or store entrances with the large single-use retail operator, whether or not such area(s) are under the same management as the large single-use retail operator. (Chandler, Arizona)

Chandler's definition has two parts. The first part defines a large-scale retail use; the second part specifies what is included in the building coverage. A city should have a consistent definition of building coverage that applies to all buildings and not just a single type of retail.

Definitions employing a criterion other than size or product type. Within the definitions for the large general merchandise and superstore, local governments have expressed a concern for these establishments' competition with local grocery retailers. Aside from defining the percent of gross leasable area dedicated to the sale of nontaxable items (such as groceries), another approach is to define a big-box retailer by its inventory size or number of "stock keeping units" (SKUs).

An SKU describes a retailer's inventory. A product in a particular style from a particular manufacturer is given a single SKU; for example, a "large" shirt from a single manufacturer gets a single SKU. Different retailers can be characterized by different SKUs; for example, warehouse clubs have a relatively small number of SKUs (between 3,500 and 4,500) with large stock within each SKU. Big-box stores have a much higher number of SKUs (between 50,000 and 200,000) but don't carry as much stock for each. Traditional supermarkets have about 25,000 SKUs. Using SKUs to define big-box stores and superstores may provide greater distinctions between types of retailers than can be captured through size regulations.

San Diego, California, used SKUs in proposing a definition for superstore, coupling it with a size criterion:

> **superstore** [A retail store] 130,000 square feet or larger, selling over 30,000 SKUs, of which at least 10 percent are nontaxable (grocery) items. All three characteristics must be present to be considered a superstore.

This definition, for example, would capture Wal-Mart and possibly Target superstores, but would exclude Costco and other bulk merchandise or warehouse clubs. Employing this definition would require retailers to periodically provide the city with SKU data. This would require review and monitoring by city staff.

Crafting definitions is challenging. Below are several recommendations for creating definitions.

- Definitions should not include development criteria, which should be left to the zoning text.

- The definition should clearly distinguish this particular retail use from other retail uses.

- Think about the variety of uses that might fit this definition and make sure this is what the city needs and wants to define. Consider that a definition simply based on size might apply to some department stores as well as big-box retailers.

The most appropriate definition will depend on how the city wants to regulate big-box retail development. For example, if the city wants to restrict the location of supercenters, a definition of a supercenter needs to be crafted. In other cases, the city may want to regulate the creation of big-box shopping centers rather than stand-alone stores. In this case, a definition might apply to retail developments with more than 250,000 square feet with one or more tenant spaces with 20,000 or more square feet.

Sources of Information about Trends in Big-Box Retail

It is very important for planners to monitor trends in big-box retail, both in terms of design innovations and business practices because the chances are good that the community's citizens will be barraged with information from both sides (pro and con) of the big-box debate. Planners may need to serve as facilitators at public meetings between proponents and opponents. Good information that can counter rumors or falsehoods is the best way to do that.

The first source for obtaining information about the retail industry should be the World Wide Web. Wal-Mart has a real estate website (www.walmart-realty.com/) that provides information on available buildings, square footage of buildings, and how their stores have been reused after closing, see Table 1 for the addresses of other retailers. Professional organizations and trade publications are also good sources for following trends in big-box retail, and many of these publications are available at no cost online. Some examples include: *Retail Traffic* (www.retailtrafficmag.com), *DSN Retailing Today* (www.dsnretailingtoday.com), and *Shopping Centers Today* (www.icsc.org).

Major magazines such as *Money* or *Newsweek* also provide information on major trends in retailing. For example, in a recent issue of *CNNMoney*, Wal-Mart announced that it plans to speed up its construction plans for new Wal-Mart stores in 2006, adding more than 60 million square feet of store space. This ramp-up in construction is because Wal-Mart CEO Lee Scott expects zoning laws to get tougher in the years ahead (CNN Money 2005).

An excellent source for information about the plans of big-box retailers is their Securities and Exchange Commission (SEC) Annual Report. The SEC provides the EDGAR system, a database of forms and filings, for searching specific SEC filings. Every publicly traded company is required to submit an annual report to the SEC. The annual report for most companies has a section on future plans for development and information about current building practices and store locations.

Consider what we were able to find in the *2004 Annual Report for Home Depot:*

- At the end of its 2004 fiscal year, Home Depot operated 1,890 stores with more than 200 million square feet under the names Home Depot and EXPO Design Center.

- In 2004, the company opened 142 new Home Depot stores in the United States and now represents 12 percent of the home improvement industry.

- Home Depot stores average 106,000 square feet of enclosed space and 22,000 square feet in the outside garden area.

- There are 54 EXPO Design Centers averaging 100,000 square feet in size. The company did not open any additional EXPO stores in 2004 and had no plans to open any in 2005.

- Home Depot's development strategy is to open new stores near the edge of market areas served by existing stores. The company admits that although opening new stores near existing stores may have a negative impact on store sales growth, they believe this "cannibalization" strategy increases customer satisfaction and overall market share.

- Currently, the company is working on three additional store formats for professional customers, including Home Depot Supply, Home Depot Landscape Supply, and the Home Depot Floor Store. There are currently 20 Home Depot Supply stores, 11 Home Depot Landscape Supply stores, and two Home Depot Floor Stores.

- The Home Depot Supply store distributes and sells installation services to businesses and government. This format operates under a variety of different names, including Apex Supply Company, Your Other Warehouse, Home Depot Supply, White Cap Industries, and HD Builder Solutions Group.

- In the 2005 fiscal year, the company plans to open 175 landscape supply stores, each averaging 12,000 square feet in covered floor area, and including a greenhouse and one to three acres of outdoor area.

This wealth of information provides insight on the big-box retailer's growth strategy and average square footage for various store formats. This information would prove useful in responding to requests for development incentives and in other interactions with the retailer.

In general, if you are a planner working on a retail-based economic development strategy, you need to know what types of retailers may be willing to locate in your area. The information from an annual report can tell you what types of areas a retailer is looking to build in.

Trends in Big-Box Retail

In general, all types of big-box retailers increased the size of their establishments in the latter part of the twentieth century. In the last decade of the 1990s, supercenters, including Wal-Mart SuperCenter, Big K, and SuperTarget, became the leading format among general merchandise retailers. Wal-Mart now has supercenters in 45 states (Wal-Mart 2005a).

Jan Evans

Figure 15. *Wal-Mart found that the 270,000-square-foot Hypermarts were just too big. This former Hypermart, in Arlington, Texas, was converted to a Wal-Mart Supercenter.*

Corrin Hoegen

Figure 16. *The first Kroger Marketplace in Columbus, Ohio.*

Jennifer Evans-Cowley

Figure 17. *A Wal-Mart Neighborhood Market in Oklahoma City.*

The trend of expansion is no longer dominated by general merchandise retailers. In 2004, Kroger introduced the 100,000-square-foot Kroger Marketplace and plans to build three more supercenters in 2005 (Kroger 2004). While supercenters held only 9.3 percent of the grocery business in 2000, this number is expected to increase throughout the early part of the twenty-first century (Gereffi 2002).

Wal-Mart is the only general merchandise retailer opening smaller stores. Wal-Mart introduced the Neighborhood Market in 1998. The stores range between 42,000 and 55,000 square feet, one-quarter the size of a Wal-Mart Supercenter, requiring a limited focus on only grocery and convenience items. Neighborhood Markets locate in the distribution shed of an existing Wal-Mart Supercenter in order to use that system. For example, in the western half of Tarrant County, Texas, there are six Neighborhood Markets. All of these stores are located within 10 miles of a Wal-Mart Supercenter. By January 2005, Wal-Mart operated 85 Neighborhood Markets, and in 2005 it planned to open 21 new Neighborhood Markets (Wal-Mart 2005).

PLANNING ISSUES CREATED BY THE BIG BOX AND ITS BUSINESS PRACTICES

The planning problems created by the presence of a big-box retailer fall into two categories. The first are what we might call traditional planning problems. Consider the photos on pages 4-5 of this report. Clearly, the traditional big-box is ugly. And there are also problems of traffic generation. The second category of problem is one concerning economic development. What effects do the big-box retail establishments have on the local economy? We will attempt to outline these problems here and suggest ways in which planners can respond to them.

The Design Issue

Big-box retail establishments, as the section above about defining the big-box makes clear, are very large. Because they are very large, they have an overwhelming aesthetic impact on a community. Big-box retailers have come to understand that sensitivity to community concerns about design is important. Just as in dealing with other design NIMBYs (for example, manufactured housing, fast-food franchises), planners and citizens are looking for alternatives to the standard or perceived design norm for these uses. And like PAS Reports before this one (see, for example, PAS 504/505 about franchise design and PAS 478 for manufactured housing design), this report offers examples of both design concerns and innovations so that a community may present its design objectives to a big-box retailer and tell it, We want something like this. There are multistory big boxes, new urbanist big boxes, and environmentally friendly big boxes. There is some overlap in the categories below (for example, multistory big-boxes might also be infill big-boxes), so read through each section to get the full panoply of innovations.

Multistory big-boxes. Historically, big-box retailers have constructed stores in suburban and exurban markets. Retailers are now looking inward towards city centers because of growing populations and the affluence of downtown residents. An urban setting often requires adapting established formats to smaller lots and higher land and labor costs. To varying degrees of financial success, retailers such as Home Depot, Wal-Mart, Toys 'R Us, and others have developed multilevel versions of their traditional store formats or introduced new store concepts with fewer product lines (e.g., Wal-Mart Neighborhood Markets, Sears Essentials). In an urban setting, greater attention is generally given on the part of local regulators to ensure that large-scale retail development is consistent with local character.

Home Depot, for instance, "took a look at the success of our stores in the Chicago area, we saw the tremendous demand in Lincoln Park. . . . We decided we could better serve our customers by designing a special store . . . [and] carefully choosing the merchandise that is in demand within the neighborhood . . ." (The Home Depot 2003). Home Depot now has urban stores in West Vancouver, Canada; Chicago; Staten Island; Manhattan; and Brooklyn. The Lincoln Park store has four-stories with 80,000 square feet: 40,000 for parking on the top two and 40,000 square feet of store space below. This is significantly smaller than the typical 106,000-square-foot Home Depot store. The store, which opened in 2003, has floor-to-ceiling glass windows, smaller signage, and other architectural features not typically seen at a Home Depot store.

Wal-Mart began building multistory stores in 1998. In Panorama City, California, it converted a 200,000-square-foot, three-story department store into a 110,000-square-foot, two-level Wal-Mart store. The remaining space is used for warehousing and offices. In Baldwin Hills, California, Wal-Mart renovated a three-story, 150,000-square-foot Macy's. The new store opened in 2001 and is part of a large shopping center that includes a Sears, Magic Johnson Theater, and Albertson's (Scally 2000). (See more about shopping centers with big-box establishments below.) In 2005, Wal-Mart opened a two-floor store in a high-rise development in Rego, New York (Goldberg 2005).

Figures 18 and 19. The Home Depot in Chicago's Lincoln Park neighborhood. The two-story glass façade fits with Chicago's urban commercial guidelines about providing a pedestrian-friendly streetfront, which is quite different from the suburban "warehouse" appearance of most Home Depot stores.

Target Corporation

Figure 20. The four-story Target Center in Minneapolis, Minnesota.

Julia Musson

Figure 21. The multistory University Heights shopping center that includes several big-box retailers on the same site.

In University Heights, Ohio, Starwood Wasserman developed a 620,000-square-foot multistory shopping center that replaces a stand-alone department center and includes several big-box retailers. The retailers are wrapped around a multilevel parking garage that allows shoppers to park on the level they plan to visit. Escalators connect the floors and also inside each store is an escalator with stairs large enough to accommodate the large shopping carts typically used by big-box retailers (Thorne 2003). Customers, after placing their cart on the escalator, walk onto an adjacent pedestrian escalator. A Kaufmann's department store is on the ground floor; a Tops supermarket is on the second floor; TJ Maxx and another part of Kaufmann's are located on the third floor; and Target is located on the third and fourth floor. David Wasserman, the developer, noted that this type of design captures one of the benefits that malls and mixed-use developments offer:

> If you think about it, it's much more convenient than shopping in a 600,000-square-foot shopping center that's spread over five acres. . . . You avoid the traffic nightmare of driving over there to the Gap . . . then on to Target . . . and the grocery store. Here you can make those five trips with one stop.

The village's mayor agrees:

> We're thrilled, because we have a development here that's going to be very productive for us and for the people that shop there. . . . It's a stunning design, and . . . it makes better use of land."

In addition to the big-box retailers, the center includes restaurants and smaller shops (Thorne 2003).

If these urban stores succeed, other big-box retailers are likely to consider urban multistory locations. For example, K-Mart currently has no multilevel stores and has no plans for multilevel stores.

Side-by-side stores. Calvert County, Maryland, passed regulations in 2004 that limited the size of big-box retailers to 75,000 square feet. Wal-Mart responded by submitting plans to build a 74,998-square-foot store with a 22,689-square-foot garden center. Wal-Mart designed each store to have its own entrance, utilities, bathrooms, and cash registers. Mia Masten, the community affairs manager for Wal-Mart's eastern region, said, "as these big-box bills come up, all retailers will just have to be flexible. . . . We developed a model that allowed us to reach our customers" (Paley 2005). Community members raised objections to the plan saying "that Wal-Mart was violating the intent of the regulations" (Gregory Bowen, e-mail correspondence with author, July 1, 2005). After community opposition, Wal-Mart decided to withdraw its plans for a side-by-side store and instead build a 75,000-square-foot store (Bowen 2005). If Wal-Mart had felt strongly about building the store and saw its plan as meeting the letter, if not the spirit, of the regulations, it might have gone to court to sidestep the county's regulations.

Home Depot has developed plans for side-by-side stores but has not yet built one. The stores would have the lumber and garden center in one store and all of the remaining items in a separate store. In the middle would be a drive-thru to service the stores (Jaime Chinnock, e-mail correspondence with author, 2005).

Power Towns. The Power Center is a shopping center with three or more big-box tenants and a few smaller tenants, 250,000 to 600,000 square feet in size, and common throughout the United States; from this evolved the Power Town. The International Council of Shopping Centers reports that customers will spend more money at Power Towns than they would spend at enclosed shopping malls (Boswell 2003). A Power Town contains between 600,000 and 1 million or more square feet of retail space on more than 80 acres of land with added open space for the customers. A Power Town typically includes three big-box stores, a movie theater or other form of entertainment, a large bookstore, and dining options.

Vestar Development Company built a prototypical Power Town, called Desert Ridge, in Phoenix, Arizona, in 2001. The 1.2-million-square-foot center includes 800,000 square feet of big-box space, including a Target Greatland, an Albertson's, a Marshall's Mega Store, an Old Navy, and a Kohl's. Amenities such as an AMC Theater, Ultimate Electronics, DSW Shoes, Barnes and Noble, Petsmart, Tower Records, and specialty retailers fill Desert Ridge, which is so large that it includes an alternative fuel-powered shuttle and five interactive fountains. Desert Ridge attracted 17 million visitors in its first year (Vestar Development 2005).

Shopping malls anchored by a big-box retailer. Shopping malls typically include a number of department stores as anchors, but this is changing. Mall owners and developers are now including big-box retailers as anchors in part because of need. Over the last few years there have been consolidations among department stores, which have resulted in store closings and an increasing need to fill anchor spaces. Richard Green, Vice Chairman of The Westfield Group, a mall developer, made it clear that times have changed for malls—"The owners of department stores and luxury stores had an attitude many years ago about this [anchoring a mall with a discount retailer, rather than a department store], but today they are saying these are the same

Figure 22. *The Barnes and Noble store in The District at Desert Ridge, a Power Town in Phoenix, Arizona.*

Figure 23. *Covered sidewalks, seating, and landscaping are some of the amenities that differentiate The District at Desert Ridge in Phoenix, Arizona, from a typical Power Town.*

customers [that shop in department stores]" (Grant 2005). Patrice Duker of the International Council of Shopping Centers confirms this, "The role of an anchor is to draw customers to a center. So when circumstances change, you have to look for uses that continue to draw people" (Goll 2004).

Costco is one example of a big-box retailer considering mall locations. Costco Chairman Jeffrey Brotman told *The New York Times*, "We have become much more known for attracting the customer they [malls] are all dying to have in an area." Costco has opened a store in the Spotsylvania Mall in Fredericksburg, Virginia (Grant 2005).

In San Diego, Wal-Mart is an anchor in the Westfield Shopping Parkway. The mall also includes Sears, Mervyn's, JCPenney, and Robinson-May as anchors. Westfield Group, a mall developer, is including big-box retailers as part of other malls as well, including a Target at the Topengo Mall in Woodland Hills, California (Grant 2005). Westfield has included Targets at eight of its malls and Best Buys at seven of its malls.

New urbanist and mixed-use projects. Cindy Steward, Director of Local Government Relations with the International Council of Shopping Centers, sums up the situation nicely:

> The suburbs are saturated, and developers and retailers are looking for new markets, and those really are old markets that may be undergoing a rebirth. And when you go out to the green space, there are a lot of growth management laws in place that make those projects more difficult to do. (Goldberg 2005)

Infill development, neighborhood development (like the urban multistory centers noted above), new subdivisions, and planned unit developments are all candidates for the current design trend.

Wal-Mart selected Atlanta to build the most urban store in the country, despite the challenge of finding an available site to accommodate a big-box retail store. "We believe this store will be representative of how retail development in urban centers should be done," wrote Michael Driver, Wal-Mart's real estate manager (Quinn 2004). Wal-Mart is working with Selig Enterprises at a 17-acre site to build a 150,000-square-foot Wal-Mart, which will include 15,000 square feet of retail shops on a second story, apartments, and 1,240 decked parking spaces, much of it hidden underground (Woods and DeGross 2004). The 280-unit apartment complex will be located next to

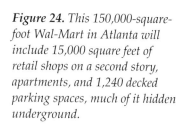

Figure 24. *This 150,000-square-foot Wal-Mart in Atlanta will include 15,000 square feet of retail shops on a second story, apartments, and 1,240 decked parking spaces, much of it hidden underground.*

Selig Enterprises

the store. The site faces I-75 on one level and Howell Mill Road on a higher level. The Wal-Mart is on the lower level. Above that, a boulevard will be built dividing the rows of shops. The boulevard will have trees, fountains, benches, bike racks, restaurants with outdoor seating, and a linear park that will lead to the apartments.

Figure 25. The use of awnings, noncontinuous facades, landscaping, and other amenities makes this Wal-Mart "development" look more like a street than a mall.

Also in Atlanta is the Edgewood Retail District, located in a historic trolley car suburb, which will incorporate new urbanism principles by including 650,000 square feet of retail and 300 apartments (Miller 2004). The Edgewood neighborhood is made up of bungalow homes and industrial areas, but lacks a commercial core. The neighborhood wanted to see new big-box retail consistent with the existing neighborhood design. The project developer, the Sembler Company, initially planned to create a typical retail power center, but after discussion with neighborhood residents, it realized a different approach would be required. The developer held a seven-day charrette to develop a site plan with neighborhood input.

The project includes a block system with tree- and sidewalk-lined streets and underground utilities. Parking is located on the interior of the blocks, hidden from the existing neighborhood. Along the perimeter, residential, retail, and mixed-use buildings create a street edge. The components include: 217 housing units, including affordable senior housing units, loft apartments, and town homes; 485,000 square feet of big-box retail, represented by Lowe's, Barnes and Noble, Bed, Bath, and Beyond, Best Buy, Kroger, Ross, and Target, and 55,000 square feet of neighborhood retail; and 15,000 square feet of second-story office space. The architectural design is Mediterranean with brick facades and tiled roofs. A 0.6-acre park is located at the center of the site and a one-acre park is located near existing housing. Additionally, the project is within one-quarter mile of two rail stations and is served by five bus routes. The project opened during the summer of 2005 (Sembler 2005).

In downtown Burnsville, Minnesota, a new mixed-use development with a large grocery store, retail, condominiums, and an office building opened in 2005. The development includes 203 condominiums and 30 townhomes. The retail building has a 68,000-square-foot grocery store and 14,000 square feet of strip center. There is a two-story office and bank building. The project is part of a 54-acre redevelopment project known as "Heart of the City" (Jenni Faulkner, e-mail correspondence with author, August 4, 2005). The project's design results from the city's 1999 design manual and zoning ordinance that outlines design standards for future development in the downtown area. Burnsville had to relocate utilities, reroute two streets, install a stormwater pond, and provide decorative intersections. The city anticipates a significant increase in tax revenues as a result of the redevelopment, increasing tax receipts from $200,000 to $4 million (Burnsville 2005).

Figure 26 (above). The 54-acre redevelopment project known as "Heart of the City" in Burnsville, Minnesota, includes 203 condominiums and 30 townhomes. The retail building has a 68,000-square-foot grocery store and 14,000 square feet of strip center. There is a two-story office and bank building. *Figure 27 (below).* The "Heart of the City" design results from Burnsville's design standards for development in its downtown. Burnsville relocated utilities, rerouted two streets, installed a stormwater pond, and provided decorative intersections as its part of the project. The city anticipates an increase in tax revenues from $200,000 to $4 million from the project.

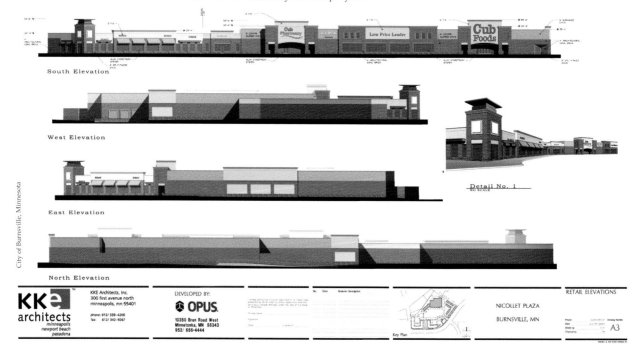

Hurricane Katrina destroyed two Wal-Marts on the Mississippi Gulf Coast. Following the hurricane, the Mississippi Governor's Commission for Recovery, Rebuilding, and Renewal, in partnership with the Congress for the New Urbanism, hosted a weeklong design charrette to explore how communities could be rebuilt. As part of the charrette, planners and architects explored turning Wal-Mart big-box stores into community stores. Ideas included placing apartments and condominiums around the store, with easy access for pedestrians. Parking would be hidden behind the building rather than in front.

Wal-Mart plans to explore these ideas during 2006. "We haven't made any commitments to these specific designs. . . . We definitely want to keep our options open," said Glen Wilkins, a Community Affairs Manager for Wal-Mart's Southeast Region (Nasser 2005).

Figure 28. A Mississippi Wal-Mart destroyed by hurricane Katrina.

Figure 29. The Mississippi Governor's Commission for Recovery, Rebuilding, and Renewal hosted a design charrette to explore ways of converting destroyed Wal-Mart big-box stores into community stores. Ideas included placing apartments and condominiums around the store, with easy access for pedestrians. Parking would be hidden behind the building rather than in front. Wal-Mart has not signed on to the idea.

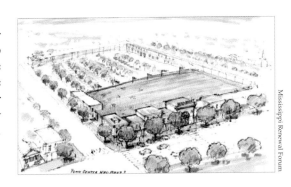

Burnsville and Atlanta aren't the only examples of big-box retail employing mixed-use and new urbanist principles. Based on the survey done for this PAS Report, more than 30 other cities have this type of development, including Chicago, Boston, Cincinnati, Tulsa, and Minneapolis.

Infill development. Big-box retailers have also been seeking out infill sites in urban areas and employing adaptive reuse of failed department stores to establish a greater urban presence. More than 30 cities responding to our survey reported some movement toward infill and adaptive reuse. Infill development and adaptive reuse benefit the community by keeping abandoned properties from becoming a problem and using existing infrastructure. The companies also cite the creation of jobs for inner-city residents, but there has been a debate about the nature of those jobs and their wages and benefits (see the section on big-box retail and economic development below).

In Ventura, California, for example, a vacant Montgomery Wards was demolished and the site was redeveloped as a Lowe's Home Improvement Store. The city's design review committee required a design that reflected the coastal California context. The new store provided a benefit to the community by redeveloping a vacant building and adding to the tax base, and it is outperforming earning expectations (Stratis Perros, e-mail correspondence with author, July 11, 2005).

Figure 30. A vacant Montgomery Wards in Ventura, California, was demolished and redeveloped as a Lowe's. The new store provided a benefit to the community by redeveloping a vacant building and adding to the tax base, and it is outperforming earning expectations.

City of Ventura, California

Figure 31. Ventura's design review process resulted in a design that reflects the city's coastal environment.

City of Ventura, California

In New Orleans, a Wal-Mart Supercenter opened in 2004 as part of a mixed-use development on the former site of the St. Thomas Public Housing site in the Lower Garden District. The 65-acre site has a Wal-Mart and 1,100 rental and owner-occupied housing units. The $318 million project was substantially funded by the public, with contributions from Hope IV, a state bond issue, and creation of a tax increment financing district. Partners included the City of New Orleans, the Housing Authority of New Orleans, and the State of Louisiana. The store was closed due to Hurricane Katrina, but will reopen in March 2006.

To accommodate the Wal-Mart Supercenter and housing, 1,500 public housing units and several warehouses were demolished. The Supercenter occupies 199,993 square feet and has 825 parking spaces (Wal-Mart 2004). The building is designed to be architecturally contextual with the Lower Garden District. This includes a corniced building in red brick similar to the historic cotton warehouses. It also includes an enclosed courtyard garden center, brick archways, and hand-painted signs (Davis 2004; Eller 2004).

Alternative architectural designs. Wal-Mart and other retailers are now providing alternatives to their standard architectural design as a response to local zoning requirements and market demand in upscale neighborhoods. "We've reached a stage where we can be flexible. We no longer have to build a gray-blue battleship box," says Robert Stoke, Senior Real Estate Manager for Wal-Mart (Goldberg 2005). Wal-Mart's new store design templates feature Main Street, Cape Cod, Adirondack, Urban Industrial, Art Deco, and Mediterranean. These stores are being built in fast-growing upscale neighborhoods to reflect the local character (Eller 2004). The Art Deco design is being debuted in Los Angeles and the Mediterranean design in West Des Moines, Iowa (Eller 2004). Alternative designs will be discussed further in the regulatory strategies section of this report.

Figure 32. This Phoenix, Arizona, Target captures some of the Southwest flavor, but the parking lot's size leaves it looking like an island.

Green design. Beyond architecturally integrated designs, big-boxes are starting to go green. McKinney, Texas, in 2005, received Wal-Mart's first new environmentally friendly supercenter. Wal-Mart built a 206,000-square-foot store that included a number of green design features. Mike Duke, the CEO of Wal-Mart Stores-USA states, "we see it as a next step in evaluating the impact we leave on the environment as we look toward smart growth and sustainability in the building of our new stores. This store will contain many of the best resource conservation and sustainable design technologies currently available to minimize the use of energy and natural resources" (Wal-Mart 2005b). According to Brian Jones (telephone conversation with author, 2005), Director of Planning for McKinney, the city has no requirements that mandated green design. Wal-Mart chose to build a green store.

The McKinney store will consume less energy, use fewer raw materials in construction, and employ renewable materials in construction. For example, the waste cooking oil used in the kitchen will be mixed with automotive oil from the Tire and Lube Express to heat the building. The store features a retention pond that collects runoff used to irrigate the landscaping. Five percent of the store's energy comes from wind and solar power; the rooftop includes a 120-foot wind turbine (Associated Press 2005). Wal-Mart claims to be the only company in America that has committed to offset its footprint for land conservation. They are preserving an acre of wildlife habitat for every developed acre (Wal-Mart 2005b). Wal-Mart plans to open another environmentally friendly store in Aurora, Colorado (Associated Press 2005).

Whole Foods is one of several grocery stores that are constructing Leadership in Energy and Environmental Design (LEED)-certified stores. Whole Foods opened the first LEED-certified grocery store in 2004 in Sarasota Springs, Florida. Since then, Giant Eagle has constructed a LEED-certified store in Brunswick, Ohio, in 2004 and a store in Pittsburgh in 2005, and Safeway opened a store in a mixed-use facility in downtown Portland that has applied for LEED certification. These grocery chains are giving new meaning to the term green grocer).

The LEED Green Building Rating System is a voluntary, consensus-based national standard for developing sustainable buildings. Members of the U.S. Green Building Council representing all segments of the building industry developed LEED standards. In order to receive LEED certification, buildings must be constructed to receive points based on a number of factors including water efficiency, use of energy, access to transportation, indoor environmental quality, reuse of building materials, and paving. For more information on the LEED System, visit www.usgbc.org.

REI, a sporting goods store, is another big-box retailer voluntarily constructing all of its stores with "green" building principles in mind. REI's Seattle store has carbon monoxide sensors that activate exhaust fans in the 475-car garage only when needed. The building was sited to optimize solar energy collection and uses elevators instead of escalators to reduce energy consumption. Recycled materials are used throughout the building and landscaping. The store site includes bike racks and a shower to encourage employees to bike to work, and a covered bus stop for public transportation users (Nadel 1999).

Figure 33. REI, a sporting goods store, is another big-box retailer voluntarily constructing all of its stores with "green" building principles in mind. REI's Seattle store has carbon monoxide sensors that activate exhaust fans in the 475-car garage only when needed, solar energy collectors, bike storage, showers for bike riders, and uses recycled materials throughout the building and landscaping.

Figure 34. REI's Portland store is the first retail building in the country to receive the LEED Gold Award for Commercial Interiors. The 37,500-square-foot store occupies the first two floors of a 10-story mixed-use building, with residential lofts above.

REI's recently completed Portland store is the first retail building in the country to receive the LEED Gold Award for Commercial Interiors. The 37,500-square-foot store occupies the first two floors of a 10-story mixed-use building, with residential lofts above. The building includes recycled materials, low-water-use fixtures, and natural light. This outdoor sports company understands that its customers value their green building principles (REI 2004).

Gas stations as part of the big-box makeup. Big-box retailers tend to sell gasoline at a reduced price, between three and seven cents per gallon less than conventional service stations (Wall Street Journal 2005). Kroger began selling gas in 1998 and operates hundreds of fuel centers. BJ's Wholesale Club operates gas stations at 81 of its 157 stores. According to Energy Analysts International, in 2002, 5.9 percent of gas sales occurred at grocery stores. This figure could grow to 12 percent by 2008 as more retailers add fuel stations (RetailTraffic 2005).

Figure 35. In 2002, 5.9 percent of all gas sales occurred at grocery stores. By 2008, that figure may rise to as much as 12 percent. There are implications for design that planners should take into account.

Mark Dotzour

While grocers and general merchandise retailers were the first to add gas stations, specialized retailers are following suit. Home Depot is now experimenting with convenience stores and gas stations. In late 2005, the company will open convenience stores with gas stations at four locations in Nashville, two of which will include car washes. If the pilot program is successful, convenience stores with gas stations could be added to many of the other Home Depot stores across the country (RetailTraffic 2005).

As oil prices have risen significantly in 2004/2005, planners should be aware that consumers are likely to turn to the places that offer the lowest prices more than ever. In other words, this is a trend to watch closely and to make sure one's community has design and regulatory standards in hand when a proposal for the establishment of a gas station in a big-box parking lot comes into the department.

The drive-thru big-box. Big-box retail is considering a new type of development that could arrive in communities in the next 10 years. AutoCart has designed a 100,000-square-foot big-box store designed as a drive-thru building. The drive-thru superstore would allow customers in up to 600 vehicles per hour purchase groceries, office supplies, and other products from 30 stations in the store by driving into the building and circulating through aisles to the stations where they need goods. AutoCart plans to open its first store in 2006 in the Southwest (AutoCart 2005). Clearly, this is one new type of development planners and citizens need to consider carefully. Imagine a drive-thru establishment on this scale. If a community were to decide to accept one of these developments, issues of queuing, traffic management, site design, environmental effects, and more would need to be addressed on a much larger scale than is normal for drive-thru establishments.

Figure 36. *Imagine, if you can, a drive-thru big-box store. This illustration gives one some idea of how that might work.*

Local Economic Development and the Big-Box Business

Even if a big-box establishment is ugly, some people will love its presence in the community because of its lower prices. While the innovations that many big-box retailers are making in design may help resolve or mitigate design concerns, the issue of a big-box's effect on the local economy, both in terms of its overall effect on wages and its overall effect on employment, has risen to the forefront of community debate. As noted at the very beginning of this report, issues of employee wages and benefits are usually outside the purview of most planning departments, but if planners are involved in the decision-making process about economic development practices, these findings have a bearing on how planners might best educate their constituents about all the economic impacts of a big-box retailer and serve as facilitators between competing groups within the community.

The positive side of big-box retail. Big-box retailers provide necessary products to consumers at low prices. Low-income residents might be especially well served by big-box retailers; frankly, affordability can be a major selling point in any community. In some urban neighborhoods that lack sufficient local retail stores (e.g., grocery), big-box retailers help fill a void. In the case of Wal-Mart, which has been more heavily studied than any other big-box retailer, research has shown a basket of groceries from a Wal-Mart supercenter was as much as 17 to 29 percent less than the same basket purchased in a major supermarket chain in 2002 (Goldman and Cleeland 2003). More generally, Global Insight (2005) estimates that between 1985-2004, Wal-Mart pricing alone led to a 9.1 percent reduction in food-at-home prices, a 4.2 percent decline in the price of goods other than groceries, and a 3.1 percent decline overall in consumer prices.

And these retailers indisputably create jobs. Big-box retailers usually hire hundreds of employees per store. Wal-Mart, for example, projects it will create more than 100,000 jobs in 2005, up from 83,000 created in 2004 in the United States (Wal-Mart Facts 2005c). For communities with high unemployment rates, such promise is hard to turn away. Some big-box retailers, like Costco, have been able to create good jobs in the large-retail sector. (See sidebar.) Others, especially Wal-Mart, have become tarred with the image of the low-pay, low-benefit employer (see the following section).

COSTCO BUCKS THE TREND IN BIG-BOX EMPLOYEE WAGES AND BENEFITS

Costco has been sited for its differences in operation from Wal-Mart and its closest competitor, Sam's Warehouse Club, a division of Wal-Mart. Several statistics stand out about Costco:

- Costco pays an average wage of $16 per hour compared to the $9.68 per hour average at Wal-Mart.

- Only 18 percent of Costco's employees are unionized (a total of 15,000 employees), but the presence of the union helps determine labor standards for all and has a positive effect on wages and benefits.

- Sales at Costco average $795 per square foot versus $516 at Sam's Warehouse Club, a division of Wal-Mart.

- Health care benefits offered by Costco are "better-than-average" for the large-retail sector; between 80 and 90 percent of its workforce has those benefits.

- Costco's employee turnover rate is less than half of Wal-Mart's. The savings in hiring and training are significant. As quoted in Herbst (2005, 2), Eileen Appelbaum, a professor in Rutgers University's School of Management and Labor Relations, says those costs are approximately $2,500 to $3,000 per year per employee lost and new hires. For Wal-Mart, that means an additional $1.5 million to $2.0 million in costs per year.

Some argue that Costco can offer greater wages and benefits because of its $45 membership fee. With 25 million members, there is more than $1 billion in fees available to the business before taking into account sales; we must note, however, that Sam's is also a warehouse club with membership fees too, and its wages and benefits are not comparable. Costco also does not advertise, saving substantial revenue. Costco offers fewer items for sale, stocking approximately 4,000 items per store as opposed to Wal-Mart's 100,000 items. Costco also offers "higher-end" products, and its shoppers are definitely more affluent than Wal-Mart shoppers. Finally, one fact that did not escape our notice: Jim Sinegal, Costco's CEO, is paid only $350,000 per year—quite a contrast to the $5.3 million paid to Wal-Mart's CEO and salaries of CEOs of companies similar in size to Costco (he's not "poor," of course; he holds more than $150 million in Costco stock).

Despite the fact that Wall Street criticizes the Costco model, Sinegal told ABC's 20/20 program (December 2, 2005):

Wall Street is in the business of making money between now and next Tuesday. We're in the business of building and organization, an institution that we hope will be here 50 years from now. And paying good wages and keeping your people working with you is very good business.

Soucres: http://abcnews.go.com/2020/Business/story?id=1362779 ; Herbst 2005.

The types of jobs in a community determine the quality of the local economy. If a local economy is heavily dependent on retail jobs, the overall quality of the economy will be low, due to the low wages produced by retail jobs.

Big-boxes generate sales tax revenue. In 2004, Wal-Mart collected $11.2 billion for state and local governments through sales taxes (Wal-Mart Facts 2005c). For communities with a small tax base, big-box retailers can sometimes mean a significant increase in the sales and property taxes paid within a community. Some cities believe that if they do not allow a big-box retailer into their community, they will experience a loss in sales tax revenue due to leakage to other communities. Such competition leads to the use of economic incentives and competition between communities to land a big-box retailer.

The shortcomings of big-box retail as an economic development tool. Some communities rejoice in job creation without giving much thought to the kinds of jobs created. Wal-Mart has been soundly criticized by labor unions, politicians, and community groups for its business practices as regards to wages and benefits. The types of jobs in a community determine the quality of the local economy. If a local economy is heavily dependent on retail jobs, the overall quality of the economy will be low, due to the low wages produced by retail jobs.

> There is nothing wrong with having retail in the economy…but the act of purchasing drains wealth from the area. Retail is absolutely dependent upon the condition of the local economy. It cannot grow any greater than the amount of disposable income within the economy. It will decline if the flow of money into an area is reduced. It does not create wealth but absorbs wealth. A vibrant, dynamic retail sector is not the cause of a strong local economy, but the result of it. (Fruth 2003, 9)

If those retail wages are even lower than normal, which is the case with wages paid by many big-box retailers as compared with other local wages, the overall negative effect on the economy may be greater than any positive effect on prices (for example, see Boarnet et al. 2005 for a comparison of Wal-Mart wages with regional wages for grocery store employees in California; Dube and Wertheim 2005, which compares Wal-Mart's wages against wages in retail overall, discount and department stores, and supermarkets). Table 2 provides a good general comparison of wages at the most visible target of research on wages and benefits, Wal-Mart, and at other retailers in various sectors. As the authors of the table note, however, "The lack of public data on wages at the corporate level makes it difficult to compare Wal-Mart's wages to those of their competition" (Dube and Wertheim 2005, 3), and these figures should be used with caution.

TABLE 2. COMPARISON OF AVERAGE HOURLY WAGES

Adjusted Average Wage	Wal-Mart Wage	Difference	% Difference
Large Retail	$11.08	$9.68	$1.40	14.5%
All Retail	10.88	9.68	1.20	12.4
Large Grocery	11.37	9.68	1.69	17.5
All Grocery	10.41	9,68	0.73	7.5
Large General Merchandise	10.41	9.68	0.73	7.5
All General Merchandise	10.44	9.68	0.76	7.9
Large General Merchandise*	12.16	9.68	2.48	25.6
All General Merchandise*	11.36	9.68	1.68	17.4

*Not including Wal-Mart employees.

Sources: Dube and Wetheim 2005, 4; 2005 March Current Population Survey (hourly workers); www. walmartfacts.org

Also consider the following, gathered from a number of independent sources. Again, the focus is on one big-box retailer that also happens to be the largest and most aggressive in its expansion campaign, Wal-Mart:

- For a 200-employee Wal-Mart Store, the Democratic Staff of the Committee on Education and the Workforce estimates a cost to federal taxpayers of $420,750 per year (Democratic Staff 2004). Wal-Mart rebuts this argument by stating that many of its employees are coming off of welfare and other social benefits when they get jobs at Wal-Mart (CNBC 2005). Most of the social benefits are paid at the state and federal level, but local communities also feel these effects through expenditures in the city or county health department, affordable housing programs, and public transit (Houston et al. 2004). Some cities and states are examining these effects and putting in place regulations to ensure benefit levels.

- At the county level, Neumark, Zhang, and Ciccarella (2005) estimate that the presence of a Wal-Mart store may reduce local employment in the retail sector by 2 to 4 percent and payroll per worker by, perhaps, as much as 3.5 percent. Either way, retail earnings fall. This same study noted that in the South, where Wal-Mart store are most prevalent and have the longest tenure, the evidence indicates that Wal-Mart reduces retail employment, total employment, and total payrolls per person.

Increases in sales tax revenues might also fall short of expectations. For example, if the store is able to increase the number of people outside the community that will now come into the community to shop or if the new store will prevent people from leaving the community to shop, there can be an increase. If not, tax revenues will remain relatively the same as there is a finite amount of money to spend within a community, and it will just shift from existing local retailers to the big-box store. Consider the following from Stone et al. (2002) in a study of the economic impact of Wal-Mart supercenters in Mississippi:

- Sales gains for Wal-Mart supercenters have been shown to correspond to losses for existing businesses in the trade area.

- The presence of a Wal-Mart supercenter has resulted in a 19 percent sales decline in other grocery stores in the county.

- Building materials stores in host counties lost between 8.2 and 14.9 percent of sales during the first five years after a supercenter opens (Stone et al. 2002).

An earlier study conducted by Kenneth Stone in Iowa found that three years after a Wal-Mart opening, retail sales in the host community began to decline, with 25 percent of the host communities experiencing sales levels below what they were before Wal-Mart arrived. This decline was often attributable to the opening of an additional Wal-Mart or other large-scale general merchandise store in the same region.

The market strategy of big-box retailers is to saturate a retail market so that stores are equally spaced to ensure that all consumers in a market area have a store convenient to them. The "shopping shed" is generally three to five miles in radius. One concern about big-box retail is that the size of the store and its sales can instantly oversaturate the market. Some communities, for example, will not be able to support a K-Mart, Wal-Mart, and Target. In such a case, one or more stores may close, leaving behind a vacant prop-

One concern about big-box retail is that the size of the store and its sales can instantly oversaturate the market. Some communities, for example, will not be able to support a K-Mart, Wal-Mart, and Target.

erty not suitable for anything but another big-box. There are provisions to help prevent the "white elephant" phenomenon, and we provide those below.

TABLE 3. SIZE COMPARISON OF BIG-BOXES AND TRADITIONAL RETAIL

Businesses	Comparative Size
Superstores	3 times the traditional supermarket
Home Depot	18 times the traditional hardware store
Chapters	12 times the traditional bookstore
Business Depot	5 times the traditional office supply store
Sports Authority	6 times the traditional sporting goods store

Source: *The Impact of Big-box Retail on Toronto's Retail Structure*

Besides competition, other big-box retail practices help create vacant stores that can become community eyesores. Big-box retailers typically stay in one location for a relatively short period of time.

Besides competition, other big-box retail practices help create vacant stores that can become community eyesores. Big-box retailers typically stay in one location for a relatively short period of time. Big-box retailers often negotiate leases that allow them to leave the building, while continuing to maintain the lease on the store and parking. The Los Angeles City Attorney reports that this practice:

> facilitates a pattern of superstores locating in a community, engaging in predatory pricing that drives out competitors, consolidating their operations by shutting down stores once competition is eliminated, and then tying up the massive parcels they have assembled through long-term leases that prevent the reestablishment of rival retailers and the recycling of industrial and commercial property. This ultimately results in declining property values for the surrounding community as a hulking vacant structure sits on an enormous parcel attracting graffiti and debris. (Los Angeles 2003, 5)

These vacant structures are a serious problem in many communities, especially because of their size and the cost of adaptive reuse of such structures. In the Kansas City metropolitan area, vacant big-box retail buildings accounted for more than half of the vacant commercial property in the area in 2000 (RH Johnson Company 2000). This report has a section starting on page 51 about how these buildings can be adapted to other uses and how cities can require a fee to assist in redeveloping vacant property.

Communities also express concern over whether a new big-box store will be there for the long term. What is the current life span for big-boxes? Christopher Thalmann, a Site Development Manager for Lowe's reports:

> It's easy to place a lifespan on how long our building and site improvements will last. We design our buildings and site improvements to last a minimum of 20 years before substantial maintenance will be required. It is much more difficult to place a lifespan on a concept. How long a lifespan did the designers of the LP and 8-track cassette tape predict? How about the designers of the phonograph or the trolley car? All are still in use, but not as widely as when they were cutting-edge technology (Thalmann 2005).

The hedging in Mr. Thalmann's quote should give communities reason to make sure abandoned big-box establishments in need of "substantial maintenance" do not dot the community's retail landscape.

Encouraging the Big Box through Economic Development Incentives

Some municipal governments welcome big-box retail establishments with tax subsidies or through the provision of infrastructure. For municipalities that rely on a sales tax as a major source of revenue, big-box retailers, in some cases, have made a significant contribution to the city's tax base. Some cities are using tax incentives for big-box retailers to encourage the redevelopment of neighborhoods and commercial corridors in urban areas and inner-ring suburbs. These incentives include the following:

- Land acquisition or assembly

- Sales tax rebate

- Development fee waiver

- Tax Increment Financing (TIF)

- Property tax abatement

- Job creation tax credits

As will be clear from the following paragraphs, these incentives are often used in combination. Government watchdog groups express concern that the majority of these development subsidies are in the form of *foregone* municipal revenue and not in the form of budget line items; therefore they are not publicly discussed in annual capital budget proceedings.

Tulsa, Oklahoma. Tulsa, Oklahoma, used land acquisition and TIF to encourage Home Depot to redevelop a site in the downtown area. The city created a TIF district, and its redevelopment authority acquired the industrial site and cleared-up title issues. The result was a dramatic decrease in the acquisition issues and costs for Home Depot (Stephen Carr, e-mail correspondence with author, July 15, 2005).

Lafayette, Louisiana. Lafayette offered an economic development incentive for Wal-Mart to build a supercenter. Incentives were provided because the only site available for a supercenter store had high land costs. The city was concerned that if economic development incentives were not offered, the store would move outside the city limits and result in a significant loss of tax revenue for the city because shoppers would do their shopping elsewhere.

Figure 37. Tulsa's redevelopment authority acquired the land in its downtown for this Home Depot store.

Figure 38. The former industrial building on the Tulsa site was converted into a Home Depot and smaller stores in Tulsa, Oklahoma. The project was possible through the creation of a TIF district.

Consequently, the city provided $2.3 million dollars for land acquisition for the store and for stormwater retention. Wal-Mart will incur the total expense upfront for the land and stormwater improvements. The city will contribute the land cost over time from the increase in sales tax revenue generated by the new store. Using this form of TIF, only the sales tax revenues above what the existing Wal-Mart store already generates (that is, the increment) will be rebated to Wal-Mart to pay for the incentives. There will be approximately a four-year payback period, after which these additional revenues will be available to the city to fund city services (Lafayette 2005).

The existing Wal-Mart store in Lafayette will be vacated. The city plans to combine the Wal-Mart site with a former Albertsons to create a downtown commercial district with housing. Lafayette views this area as an opportunity for revitalization (Lafayette 2005).

One concern about the use of land acquisition as an economic development incentive is the need to use eminent domain when the land is not owned already by a public entity. Although the Supreme Court, in *Kelo* (see PAS Report 535), upheld the use of eminent domain for economic development purposes, some states are passing laws that limit the use for economic development purposes.

Santee, California. Santee offered sales tax rebates to big-box retailers to assist the city in the creation of a 706-acre town center, known as the Santee Promonade. The city actively worked with the retailers residents wanted to bring in, specifically Costco, Wal-Mart, and Home Depot. The town center currently contains a 104-acre office park, 626,000 square feet of retail space, and another 110,000 square feet approved for development.

The city started the project by working with Costco in 1986 to relocate and expand their store (Santee 2005). In 1990, the Santee Community Development Commission agreed to provide a 50 percent rebate of the retail sales tax revenue generated by the Santee Wal-Mart store, up to $2.1 million (Retail Traffic 2001).

Beyond the sales tax rebate, the Santee Community Development Commission worked with Vestar Development Company to develop 50 acres of the site. The city and commission waived $1.2 million in traffic, drainage, and traffic signal impact fees; granted an 18-month deferral for another $1.3 million in traffic impact fees; and will reimburse Vestar for off-site public improvements. The development, Santee Trolley Square, will include entertainment, public space, and big-box retailers, including Target, Famous Footwear, TJ Maxx, Petsmart, and Old Navy (Santee Trolley Square 2005; Retail Traffic 2001). Santee Trolley Square opened in 2002 and is the centerpiece of the town center. In the future the site will include a public library and, adjacent to the site, a corporate office park on county-owned land (Santee 2005).

Madison, Wisconsin. Madison created a TIF district in the Allied Drive neighborhood. The area was blighted and contained a number of vacant buildings. A series of big-box retailers, including Home Depot, Cub Foods, and MC Sports, built stores in the area. The funds from the increase in tax values are being used to build a Boys and Girls Club and other neighborhood improvements. The development of the big-box retailers has led to other redevelopment, include a vacant strip mall being demolished and replaced with townhouses (R. Cnare, e-mail correspondence with author, July 14, 2005).

Cleveland-Cuyahoga County, Ohio. The city-county Port Authority formed a TIF district in University Heights, Ohio, to finance a public parking garage (Thorne 2003). The garage is used to support a 620,000-square-foot multistory shopping center that includes Target, Kaufmann's, TJ Maxx, and a Tops supermarket (Thorne 2003). This project is discussed in more detail in the Trends in Big-box Retail section above.

These approaches proved successful in helping these cities meet their development needs. In all the above-cited cases, big-box retailers were crucial in helping redevelop an area or in creating a new town center.

Economic development incentives should be used cautiously with retail development. It does not make economic sense to offer economic development incentives to retailers in particular because this often just shifts retail activity from one place to another and typically does not generate new jobs (Houston et al. 2000). Studies of the economic impact of big-box retail development describe this as a "fixed pie" or "zero-sum game theory" of consumer demand (Stone and Artz 2001). In terms of job creation, studies show that the development of a big-box retail establishment may even result in a net job *loss*, with the large-scale retailers operating at greater labor productivity than the small retailers that they have displaced or put out of business (Basker 2004; Mehta et al. 2004).

Communities may think they are able to capture new tax revenue from other jurisdictions, but this gain is only temporary. Economic development incentives for retailers should only be used, as in the cases above, where there is a redevelopment purpose.

Economic development incentives should be used cautiously with retail development.

REGULATORY STRATEGIES

There are a wide range of development regulations jurisdictions currently use, including development moratoria, limitations on types of products (especially groceries) sold by a retailer, "formula business" ordinances, design review, and building requirements, including regulation of size, parking, signage, landscaping, pedestrian and bicycle accommodations, and more. The following sections cover the variety of regulatory approaches reported by respondents to our survey. Please note the importance of articulating a policy of promoting local businesses in a community's comprehensive plan, which can provide a good foundation for these regulations. Consider the following examples from *The Hometown Advantage* (New Rules 2005):

Please note the importance of articulating a policy of promoting local businesses in a community's comprehensive plan, which can provide a good foundation for these regulations.

- The Kent County, Maryland, plan lists among its objectives "support [for] small, locally owned business" and "prevent[ion of] commercial sprawl outside the county's existing traditional commercial centers."

- The Skaneateles, New York, plan suggests "Rather than establishing competing shopping centers in the Town to provide basic goods and services, the Village commercial center…should remain the center for shopping in the community."

- And the Corvallis, Oregon, comprehensive plan states that the city should "support existing businesses and industries and the establishment of locally owned, managed, or controlled small businesses."

Moratoria

When communities are unprepared for the impact of a development, especially one that can be as significant to the existing retail sector of the community and region as a big-box, it is only reasonable to impose a temporary moratorium on this type of development. (Check your state enabling legislation to clarify the terms of a legal moratorium.) The community and its citizens should use the time "bought" with the moratorium to consider the effects of big-box development, to find a way to mitigate its negative effects, and to enhance its positive ones. This may involve review and revision of both the comprehensive plan and zoning regulations.

In 1999, Easton, Maryland, enacted a temporary moratorium on all new retail buildings greater than 25,000 square feet in size due to significant development pressures. At the time there were three large-scale commercial developments with 766,000 square feet of retail proposed. The town was concerned with maintaining its reputation as one of the finest small towns in America. At the same time, the town wanted to consider how to incorporate smart growth policies enacted by the state and county. The moratorium lasted three months (Easton 1999). In 2000, Easton adopted a big-box retail ordinance that limits all retail to no more than 65,000 square feet (Easton 2000).

Austin, Texas, placed a 45-day moratorium on the planning and building of supercenters and large retail stores over the Edwards Aquifer. The moratorium was a result of efforts by Wal-Mart to build a supercenter over the Edwards aquifer environmentally sensitive recharge zone. The moratorium was passed in order to allow the city time to draft a permanent ordinance to protect the aquifer (Inks 2003). The ban on big-box retail inside the Edwards aquifer recharge zone was passed in late 2003.

Other moratorium efforts are chronicled at www.newrules.org.

Square-Footage Limitations

Banning stores over a certain size may limit the kind of retail a city wants (e.g., department stores) and prove an ineffective means of regulating big-box stores in particular, as established in the discussion of side-by-side stores above. To get around this problem, some cities have chosen to limit big-box retail based on whether they have a grocery component, but even that has posed a problem (see the following section). Communities can also structure the definitions within their ordinances to treat retailers occupying multiple buildings as a single retail use subject to the cap. For example, see the definitions on page 9 from Hailey, Idaho; Winston-Salem, North Carolina; and Greeley, Colorado. Also consider these regulations on retail stores from Agoura Hills, California.

> SECTION. 9306. Retail stores.
>
> In all commercial districts, the gross floor area of a retail store shall not exceed sixty thousand (60,000) square feet. This limitation shall be applied as follows:
>
> A. The sixty thousand (60,000) square foot limitation shall apply to individual retail stores for which permits are sought and also to the cumulative sum of related or successive permits for retail stores that are part of a larger project, such as piecemeal additions to a building or multiple buildings on a lot or adjacent lots.
>
> B. For purposes of this section, the gross floor area of a retail store shall include gross floor area as defined in section 9120.6 and the area of all portions of the site outside of the exterior walls of buildings used for the display, storage, or sale of any goods, wares or merchandise, except that the gross floor area of a retail store shall not include exterior areas of not more than three thousand (3,000) square feet used for seasonal or temporary sales events under appropriate city permits or approvals.
>
> C. The gross floor area of adjacent stores shall be aggregated in cases where the stores (1) are engaged in the selling of similar or related goods, wares or merchandise and operate under common ownership or management; (2) share checkstands, a warehouse, or a distribution facility; or (3) otherwise operate as associated, integrated or co-operative business enterprises. (Agoura Hills, California, Ordinance No. 02-310, Section 3B, 3-5-2002)

The following examples show the range of limits that cities have used when they have chosen square-footage limitations for large retail stores. Please note the use of a cap governing the space that can be devoted to grocery items, which is covered in more detail in the following section.

Powell, Ohio, has a size cap of 65,000 square feet of usable floor area in one building. Additionally, the city allows only one user with more than 35,000 square feet in a building.

Hamden, Connecticut, and Minneapolis, Minnesota, tie a square-footage limit to a conditional use permit. Application for a conditional use permit also triggers design review. (More about design review appears below.)

> **GERMANY TAKES AN ANTI-SPRAWL APPROACH TO SIZE CONTROLS**
>
> German law in 1977 restricted the development of shopping centers and retail stores larger than 16,129 square feet (1,500 meters) to inner cities and designated areas where their impact on nearby facilities, traffic, population, and landscape could be minimized. In 1986, this threshold was lowered to apply to developments of 12,903 square feet (1,200 meters) or larger, which have a gross leasable area of approximately 8,602 square feet (800 meters). This strict control of retail size and location, in addition to competition from established German discount retailer Aldi, has hampered Wal-Mart's efforts to establish a presence in that country (Gerhard and Hahn 2005). ■

Some cities prohibit retail of a certain size in specific areas of the city. Kansas City, Missouri created a 10,000-square-foot cap in the Brookside Business District, but exempted grocery stores from the cap (Kansas City 2000).

In 2004, Turlock, California, approved amendments to the Northwest Triangle Specific Plan and Zoning Ordinance. The changes included adding a definition for big-box retail stores, requiring a conditional use permit for large-scale retail stores, and prohibiting retail stores greater than 100,000 square feet with more than 5 percent of the sales floor area devoted to grocery items. Wal-Mart, in response to the ordinance, filed suit against Turlock in state and federal court. It challenged the ordinance because it believed the ordinance would regulate competition, is not reasonably related to the public welfare, and is not exempt from the California Environmental Quality Act. The state court denied Wal-Mart's request for relief from the regulations (Beauchesne 2004).

Grocery Limitations

Respondents to our survey noted the use of limits on the size of the grocery component of a store to ensure two things: 1) that size limitations did not rule out department stores that are not big-boxes; and 2) that stores like Wal-Mart supercenters and SuperTargets do not destroy the existing grocery store businesses in a region. Wal-Mart, which reports that groceries represent on average 28 percent of the retail sales in its discount stores and supercenters, has been a target of such size limitations (Wal-Mart 2005a). In particular, this has been an issue because of the unionization of grocery workers in stores other than big-box retailers (for more on the grocery store debate, see Boarnet et al. 2005). The wages and volume of sales in the grocery-store portions of supercenters in California, in particular, has proved to pose a threat to the operations of and wages paid by grocery store chains.

- Arroyo Grande, California, limits stores to 90,000 square feet and 3 percent of the store floor area devoted to grocery sales.

- Kansas City, Missouri, limits the maximum gross floor area for groceries to 25,000 square feet per floor.

- Martinez, California, limits stores to 105,000 square feet and 10 percent of square footage devoted to grocery sales.

- Santa Maria, California, limits stores to 90,000 square feet with 8 percent devoted to grocery sales.

- Turlock, California, limits stores to 100,000 square feet with 5 percent devoted to grocery sales.

- Tucson, Arizona, limits stores to 10 percent of the gross floor area to grocery sales.

- Oakland, California prohibits *outright* any stores larger than 100,000 square feet that devote more than 10 percent of their sales floor area to nontaxable merchandise. To do this, they created a new use definition: "Large-Scale Combined Retail and Grocery Sales."

Formula Business Ordinances

A formula business is typically defined as one with more than a specified number of outlets in the United States that share common features such as merchandise, trademark, architecture, employee uniforms, or decor. These ordinances have been applied to chain restaurants and retail, and could be a triggering device for conditional use review or, perhaps most appropriately, an economic impact assessment for big-box retailers (Svete 2003).

Current anti-formula business ordinances are concentrated primarily in tourist destinations or other locales whose economies rely to a great extent on maintaining a unique local character (e.g. Sausalito and Calistoga, California, and Bristol, Rhode Island). Growing concern for the homogenization of retail caused by the proliferation of national chains (including big-box retailers) and the loss of local character makes regulations addressing this issue more politically viable in any location.

Anti-formula legislation enacted in San Francisco, California, provides perhaps the best existing model for a flexible application of anti-formula business restrictions. The San Francisco ordinance defines a formula business as "a type of retail activity or retail sales establishment which, along with 11 or more other retail sales establishments located in the United States, maintains two or more of the following features:

- A standardized array of merchandise

- A standardized façade

- A standardized décor and color scheme

- Uniform apparel

- Standardized signage or a trademark or servicemark

This type of business is prohibited in two neighborhoods of the city and allowed as a conditional use in one other neighborhood and in any area designated as a "Small-Scale Commercial" or "Neighborhood Commercial" district. If conditional review is triggered, notice is sent to all adjacent property owners, commercial tenants, and residents. The review takes into

A formula business is typically defined as one with more than a specified number of outlets in the United States that share common features such as merchandise, trademark, architecture, employee uniforms, or decor.

consideration the following: existing concentrations of formula uses; availability of similar retail uses in the district; compatibility with existing architectural and aesthetic character; existing retail vacancy rates in the district; and the existing mix of citywide-serving retail uses and neighborhood-serving retail uses in the district. Most importantly, the ordinance includes a provision to empower additional neighborhoods to propose the elimination of notice requirements for formula business development, make formula businesses a conditional use, or prohibit formula businesses altogether.

Legal challenges to anti-formula businesses have not been successful. The Fourth Appellate District Court of Appeals in California upheld a Coronado, California, anti-formula business ordinance in 2003. At issue was whether the ordinance unfairly discriminated against national chains. Because the law applied equally to locally owned versus out-of-state businesses, no such discrimination could be proved. The court found that the challenge did not show "unlawful discrimination or that the burden on interstate commerce [was] clearly excessive" (*Coronadans Organized for Retail Enhancement et al. v. City of Coronado,* 2003 Cal. App. Unpub. LEXIS 5769).

Design Review

Design review can be an effective method for ensuring that a new big-box retailer maintains and enhances local community character. Design review requires increased staff time and training for commissioners to understand how to judge design (see Hinshaw (1995) for a discussion of effective design review).

The design standards cities have applied to big-box retail stores cover color, architectural features, building materials, parking, signage, and outdoor storage, and more.

Building requirements. The typical materials, colors, and façade treatments used by big-box retailers to minimize construction costs are not what many communities want to see.

Delaware, Ohio, calls for design review of new retail in its comprehensive plan. In 2004, the city council decided to apply the following design standards to all projects larger than 100,000 square feet in gross floor area (Vince Papsidero, e-mail correspondence with author, June 24, 2004).

For these retailers, the following standards apply:

> All facades visible from adjoining properties or public streets shall include pleasing scale features of the building and encourage community integration by featuring characteristics similar to a front façade.
>
> All side of a principal building that directly face an abutting public street shall feature at least one customer entrance.

Figure 39. Design review led to a Wal-Mart that better respects its Anchorage, Alaska, mountainous background.

Figure 40. Madison, Mississippi, uses design review to achieve community ends in this Lowe's store.

Figure 41. Madison, Mississippi, design review applied to this retail center that contains a Wal-Mart.

Figure 42. Lakewood, Colorado, hired an architect to get the kind of Wal-Mart it wanted.

Facades greater than 100 feet in length shall incorporate recesses and projections a minimum of three feet in depth and a minimum of 20 contiguous feet within each 100 feet of façade length. Windows, awnings, entry areas, and arcades shall total at least 60 percent of the façade length facing a public street.

Smaller retail spaces that are part of a larger principal retail building shall be transparent between the height of three feet and eight feet above the walkway grade for no less than 60 percent of the horizontal length of the building façade. Windows shall be recessed and should include visually prominent sills, shutters, or other such forms of framing. Smaller retail spaces shall have separate outside entrances.

Building facades shall include a repeating pattern that shall include no less than three of the following elements: color change, texture change, material module change, or expression of architectural or structural bay through a change in plane no less than 12 inches in width, such as an offset, reveal, or projecting rib. At least one of these elements shall repeat horizontally. All elements shall repeat at intervals of no more than 30 feet, either horizontally or vertically.

Roof lines shall provide variations to reduce the massive scale of these structures and to add visual interest. Roof lines shall have a change in height every 100 linear feet in the building length. Parapets, mansard roofs, gable roofs, hip roofs, or dormers shall be used to conceal flat roofs and rooftop mechanical equipment from public view. Alternating lengths and designs may be acceptable and can be addressed during the Development Plan.

Predominant exterior building materials shall be of high quality. These include brick, wood, limestone, other native stone, and tinted/textured concrete masonry units. Smooth-faced concrete block, tilt-up concrete panels, or prefabricated steel panels are prohibited as exterior building materials.

Façade colors shall be of low reflectance, subtle, neutral or earth tone colors. The use of high-intensity colors, metallic colors, black or fluorescent colors is prohibited.

Building trim may feature brighter colors than façade colors, but neon tubing is prohibited.

Each principal building or tenant space shall have a clearly defined, highly visible customer entrance with a minimum of three of the following features: canopies, porticos, overhangs, recesses/projections, arcades, raised cornice parapets over the door, peaked roof forms, arches, outdoor patios, display windows, architectural details such as tile work and moldings which are integrated into the building structure and design, integral planters or wing walls that incorporate landscaped areas and/or places for sitting.

A continuous internal pedestrian walkway shall be provided from the perimeter public sidewalk to the principal customer entrance. This internal walkway must feature landscaping, benches, and other such materials/facilities for no less than 50 percent of its length.

Sidewalks shall be provided along the full length of the building along any facade featuring a customer entrance and along any facade abutting public parking areas. Such sidewalks shall be located at least six feet from the facade of the building to provide planting beds for foundation landscaping.

Primary tenant spaces that exceed 75,000 gross square feet in area shall be structurally designed to be easily divided into smaller tenant spaces.

Standing seam metal roofs are strongly preferred. (Delaware 2004)

An overlay district is one approach to regulating big-box design. Columbus, Ohio, enacted an overlay in 2002 to govern the redevelopment of the Graceland Shopping Center. A number of major tenants had vacated the center, creating a series of large empty spaces in the shopping center. A developer, the Casto Corporation, was in the process of identifying development alternatives for the site. The city's goal was to encourage a different type of development for this major commercial corridor.

The resulting overlay, passed in 2002:

- requires a 25-foot setback with up to a third of the building located five feet in front of or up to 15 feet behind the 25-foot setback;

- mandates that parking be set back at least 25 feet from High Street;

- prohibits parking between the principal building and right-of-way; and

- requires that parking be in the rear and on the side of the building.

Additionally, the city's zoning administrator can reduce the number of required parking spaces after site plan review. (The building must have frontage along at least 60 percent of the lot width. The overlay also contains provisions for landscaping, lighting, awnings, screening, and pedestrian access.) Development does not have to go through a design review committee or other review process if the design standards are met (Columbus 2002).

The city ultimately compromised its overlay standards to meet Costo's development plans for a Target store. The company requested a series of variances from the standards. The unique features include that the Target store is not facing High Street, the arterial. Instead, a strip center was constructed along the side of Target facing High Street. The Target store faces internal to the shopping center with the primary parking lot internal to the shopping center rather than out towards the street.

Figure 43. *This Target was built in an overlay district with design controls, but the developer was allowed a number of variances from those controls.*

Building design standards can be an effective way to ensure that big-box retailers meet the community's aesthetic standards. The standards should be specific in order to provide adequate guidance to the developer. The design standards if put in place should be specific; if materials are approved specifically, they should be inspected before being placed on the building.

Parking. Big-box retailers usually want as much parking directly in front of the store as possible. The reasoning is that they feel shoppers want to park as close to the store entrance as possible, and this has been the traditional orientation of entrance to parking lot. As you'll see below, some cities are requiring different placement of the lot, limits on the amount of parking in front of the store, or screening of the parking by outlot development and landscaping.

Survey respondents noted that big-box retailers typically choose to provide more parking than is required under the code. This is not a good thing. Retailers often build, or are often required to build, enough parking to satisfy demand for the busiest shopping day of the year. In general, parking requirements are not based on any meaningful observation and should be reexamined, especially for uses with such overwhelming impacts on design, efficient land use, and environmental degradation from stormwater volume and pollution (Shoup 2004). The discussion that follows moves from general requirements to some of the innovative approaches in the placement and screening of parking to the design of the lots themselves, as established by the respondents to our survey.

While some cities have developed parking requirements specific to large-scale retail, such as Augusta, Georgia, which requires five spaces per 1,000 square feet of gross leasable area (Augusta 2005), others use their general retail parking requirements. (For a range of parking requirements, see PAS Report 510/511; for a better way to think about parking requirements, see Shoup 2005.)

Fort Collins, Colorado, restricts the placement of parking for big-box retail. Their ordinance specifies, "no more than 50 percent of the off-street parking area for the entire property shall be located between the front facade of the principal building and the primary abutting street" (Fort Collins 1995). It also places a cap on parking equal to 125 percent of the city's minimum parking requirement (Duerksen 2005). In other words, the regulations limit both the placement and amount of parking.

Other local jurisdictions have similar restrictions. The Georgetown-Scott County Planning Commission in Kentucky specifies "no more than 60 percent of the off-street parking area for the entire property shall be located between the front façade within the front yard of the principal building(s) and the primary abutting street unless the principal building(s) and/or parking lots are screened from view by outlot development (such as restaurants) and additional tree plantings and/or berms" (Georgetown-Scott Planning Commission n.d.). Delaware, Ohio has the same limitation (Delaware 2004). Queen Creek, Arizona, and Greeley, Colorado, both mandate that no more than 75 percent of parking be located in the front of the store (Queen Creek 1999; Greeley 2005).

Some cities go beyond specifying the amount of parking allowed in front and have design standards for parking. (See Smith (1988) for more about the aesthetics of parking.) Moline, Illinois, for example, breaks up the parking lot into "pods" with landscaping requirements for each portion of the lot:

> All required off-street parking spaces and access drives shall be located entirely within the boundaries of the group development; parking design shall employ interior landscaped islands with a minimum of 400 square feet at all parking aisle ends and to provide a minimum of one landscaped island of a minimum of 400 square feet in each parking isle for every 20 cars in the aisle; aisle-end islands shall count toward meeting this requirement; landscaped medians shall be used to break large parking areas into distinct pods with a maximum of 100 spaces in one pod; a minimum of one 200-square-foot cart return area shall be provided for every parking area pod; there shall be no exterior cart return nor cart storage areas located within 25 feet of building in areas located between building and public street. (Moline 2005)

The Toledo, Ohio, standards break up a single lot into at least two pieces, specify the maximum number of spaces in each parking area with options for other types of partitions, and require buffering in some cases:

In general, parking requirements are not based on any meaningful observation and should be reexamined, especially for uses with such overwhelming impacts on design, efficient land use, and environmental degradation from stormwater volume and pollution.

Parking is to be distributed around large buildings on not less than two sides to shorten distance to other buildings and public sidewalks, to reduce perceived scale of paved surfaces; no single parking area shall exceed 200 spaces unless divided into two or more sub-areas separated from each other by landscaping, access drives or public streets, pedestrian walkways or building; if more than 65 percent of the total off-street parking spaces for entire site are located between the front facade of principal building and the Primary Street abutting the site additional landscaping, buffering and raised pedestrian walkway connection are required as conditional of approval. (Toledo 2005)

Another issue related to parking is the overnight parking of recreation vehicles. Wal-Mart is famous for allowing recreational vehicles to park overnight in their parking lot. Some cities take exception to this and have passed regulations that do not allow overnight parking of RVs. For example, Chandler, Arizona, prohibits "overnight parking of recreational vehicles anywhere within site development" (Chandler 2005).

If a city receives resistance to downsizing its parking requirements for a big-box retailer, it might be able to negotiate to provide for overflow parking. In such a case, a good alternative for environmental, aesthetic, and economic reasons is to create "green" overflow parking. Reinforced turf includes a sub-base that allows support of heavy wheel loads and high traffic volume. The turf is a series of interlocking grids of rings that hold the sand and topsoil below and the turf on top. The turf is mowed just like normal grass and can be plowed for snow at a raised level (Invisible Systems 1996). Home Depot uses this turf at its Enfield, Connecticut, store (Merriam 2005).

Figure 44. Reinforced turf, which has metal rings within it, can accommodate some retail parking and reduce the amount of impervious surface devoted to parking on the site.

Figure 45. The turf is strong enough to allow parking for heavy trucks.

In another example, West Hartford and Farmington, Connecticut, denied a 310,000-square-foot expansion of the Westfarms Mall for environmental reasons (NEMO n.d.). Green paving and additional landscaping (more than 800 trees) were enough to convince opponents to the expansion that the development would be more environmentally friendly and aesthetically pleasing. The green paving was used to create overflow parking for 700 vehicles. One important note about maintenance: the reinforced turf works well enough in providing pervious surface that the existing stormwater system did not have to be enlarged to accommodate the additional parking, making this green infrastructure at its best.

Signage

Big-box retailers, like most retailers, want large signs that are easily visible from roadways. In addition, these retailers want to include their trademarked logos to advertise their store.

The Lanham Act limits local government's ability to alter the appearance of a trademark. Courts are split on whether local governments can require a big-box retailer to alter its trademark on signage to conform to a sign regulation. In *Blockbuster Videos, Inc. v. the City of Tempe, Arizona,* the court held that a sign regulation requirement that requires a change in color for a sign constituted an alteration of the trademark under the Lanham Act. However, in a separate court case in New York, the court found that the Lanham Act was not intended to interfere with municipal aesthetic regulations (Morris 2002). Given the split decisions by the courts, regulating trademark images and colors may cause litigation against the municipal government until the Supreme Court has occasion to clarify the extent of the application of the Lanham Act.

Most cities do not single out big-box retail in their sign regulations, but rather have regulations that apply to all types of development. That said, four of the cities responding to our survey developed sign standards specific to big-box retail. Please note that when using terms like "sympathetic," "relates well," "in good taste," "coordinated and complimentary," as is the case for some of the ordinances we received and reviewed, the regulations should be supplemented with photo "definitions" of what is meant by those terms so that applicants can respond appropriately. The problem with such terms is their subjectivity, which can be contested in court.

Deltona, Florida, requires that big-box retailers comply with the existing sign code and layers on an additional set of requirements. The color and material of each sign must be "compatible" with the architecture on the site. The sign:

> shall be designed as a sympathetic architectural element of the buildings to which it is principally related; freestanding signs should have landscaping at their bases; commercial centers should have a project name that is easy to identify, relates well to the site, is not similar to other project names, does not result in any public safety issues, is in good taste and is approved by Department of Development Services and can be integrated with site identification signage to provide unified theme. (Deltona 2004)

Moline, Illinois, requires that a conceptual signage plan be provided as part of the special use application. The sign is expected to include:

> coordinated and complimentary exterior sign location, configurations, and colors throughout the planned development; all freestanding signage within the development shall complement the on-building signage; freestanding sign materials and design shall compliment building exterior and may not exceed maximum height requirement of zoning ordinance. (Moline 2005)

Similarly, Bend, Oregon, requires that a signage plan be approved. Bend provides a color guide that includes samples of approved and prohibited colors. The requirements are identical to citywide requirements except that:

> pole signs are prohibited; ground mounted signs shall not exceed 15 feet in height and 8 feet in width; wider signs may be allowed provided that the total sign area does not exceed 120 square feet; all sign bases shall be constructed of materials compatible with the architecture of buildings located on the premises; white, ivory and yellow backgrounds of internally illuminated signs shall not exceed 20 percent of the total sign area including reader boards. (Bend 2005)

Virginia Beach, Virginia, requires:

> the style, size, color and building material of all signs on site should be coordinated, including signs for any out parcel development, on-site directional signs and signs to be located in the face of any structure; colors and materials should be in keeping with the colors used on the primary structures and they should be primarily neutral or earth tone (no primary colors); a limited amount of brighter accents (primary colors), such as those found in corporate logos are acceptable; ideally, any freestanding sign associated with a retail use should be monument style with a maximum height of 8 feet; a minimum of 75 square feet of landscaping, consisting of at least 50 percent evergreens shall be included at the base of the sign; sign materials should be durable, attractive and coordinated with those used on primary structures. (Virginia Beach 2004)

Figure 46. Broomfield, Colorado, was able to negotiate with Wal-Mart to have this store use red signage rather than the company's traditional white-and-blue signage.

Sign standards should be consistent with the standards required for other types of uses. However, it may be appropriate to develop sign standards for shopping centers in order to create consistency within a major development project. Another option is to develop design standards that apply to a specific commercial corridor. Many cities already have sign regulations in place that address all types of development, but some cities may consider developing standards specific to major retail projects.

Landscaping

Big-box retailers are known for their large building and parking lots. A general lack of green space and landscaping is a concern of many cities. For most cities, the citywide landscaping requirements also apply to big-box retailers. However, some cities have developed standards specific to big-box retail sites.

Moline, Illinois, requires that the landscaping meet city code but additionally requires 1.5 times the code-required landscaping in paved areas and around the building foundation (Moline 2005).

Queen Creek, Arizona, requires a 30-foot-wide landscaped buffer to be provided along front property line and along all abutting arterial roadways with breaks for approved access. Additionally, where the facade faces adjacent residential uses, it should contain, at a minimum, evergreen trees planted at intervals of 20 feet on center or in clusters. A minimum of 20 percent of parking areas is to be landscaped, with no parking space located more than 100 feet from a landscaped area, and landscaped planters are to be provided at a minimum of one for every 10 parking spaces.

Storage

Many big-box retailers use outdoor display and storage areas. For example, at hardware stores it is common to see storage buildings, riding lawnmowers, and other items outside of the store. Many communities have regulations in place that address outdoor storage and screening.

Queen Creek, Arizona, requires that storage areas and equipment:

> shall be incorporated into overall design of building and landscape plan and views shall be screened from visibility from all property lines and separated from pedestrian areas and screening structures shall be made of same materials as principal structure; to greatest extent possible, mechanical appurtenances shall be located within the structure and external ones shall be screened and finished to match colors of adjacent building materials; these areas to be located in rear of lot and when not possible then the side yard can be used but in no case shall such areas be located within 20 feet of and shall not be visible from any public street, public sidewalk or internal walkways; shall be incorporated into overall design of building and landscape plan and views shall be screened from visibility from all property lines and separated from pedestrian areas. (Queen Creek, 2005).

In Kentucky, the Georgetown-Scott County Planning Commission specifies the following in regards to outdoor storage:

> Areas for outdoor storage, truck parking, trash collection or compaction, loading, or other such uses shall not be visible from public or private rights-of-way.

> No areas for outdoor storage, trash collection or compaction, loading, or other such uses shall be located within 20 feet of any public or street, public sidewalk, or internal pedestrian way.

> Loading docks, truck parking, outdoor storage, utility meters, HVAC equipment, trash dumpsters, trash compaction, and other service functions shall be incorporated into the overall design of the building and the landscaping so that the visual and acoustic impacts of these functions are fully contained and out of view from adjacent properties and public streets, and no attention is attracted to the functions by the use of screening materials that are different from or inferior to the principal materials of the building and landscape.

> Non-enclosed areas for the storage and sale of seasonal inventory shall be permanently defined and screened with walls and/or fences. Materials, colors, and designs of screening walls and/or fences and the cover shall conform to those used as predominant materials and colors of the building. If such areas are to be covered, then the covering shall conform to those used as predominant materials and colors on the buildings.

> Temporary sales/displays, such as Christmas trees, landscape materials, and fireworks, shall follow all outdoor requirements for B-2, B-4, and B-5 districts as described in the Zoning Ordinance. Location and time/duration of such sales/displays shall be reviewed and approved by the Planning Director or appointed designee.

Some communities find that rooftop mechanicals pose a particular aesthetic challenge. Tucson, Arizona, requires:

roof or ground mounted mechanical equipment shall be screened to mitigate noise and views in all directions; if roof mounted, screen shall be designed to conform architecturally with design of building whether it is with varying roof planes or parapet walls; wood fence or similar treatment is not acceptable; locate at least 200 feet from any residential use/zone; screen required so not visible from streets, sidewalks, internal sidewalks, adjacent residential that is 8 feet and masonry, confining noise, loose papers, cartons, trash; storage materials should not be visible above screen; best to place areas between buildings. (Tucson 2005)

Virginia Beach, Virginia, requires that "parapets must conceal all rooftop equipment such as heating, ventilation and air conditioning (HVAC) units from typical street level view; such parapets should feature 3-D cornice treatment not a 2-D superficial treatment" (Virginia Beach 2005).

Chandler, Arizona, has requirements that address the shopping cart containment areas. Their ordinance specifies:

> Any areas used for shopping cart containment as may be provided adjacent to building shall be fully enclosed and screened by a minimum of four-foot-high masonry wall, with berming and landscaping in quantities set forth in 35-1903 of Municipal Code. (Chandler 2005)

Community Amenities

Big-box retail is typically designed to encourage customers to drive, park, shop, and then leave. Communities increasingly are asking big-box retailers and shopping center developers to include community amenities as part of the development in order to create a more aesthetically pleasing development and provide spaces for people to interact outside of the store. These amenities vary from fountains to parks to clock towers.

Delaware, Ohio, requires each retail development to provide public space by providing at least two community amenities. Developers can choose to provide a patio/seating area, pedestrian plaza with benches, outdoor play area, kiosk area, water feature, clock tower, steeple, or other such deliberately shaped area and/or a focal feature or amenity that adequately enhances such community and public spaces. These amenities are required to be connected to the public sidewalk (Delaware 2004).

Queen Creek, Arizona, also requires developers to include two community amenities choosing from patio/seating area, a pedestrian plaza with benches, a window-shopping walkway, outdoor playgrounds, kiosk area, a fountain/water feature, or a clock tower. Developers are required to connect these amenities "with the remainder of community; bus stops, drop-off and pick-up points to be integrated with traffic patterns on site; special design features should enhance building's function as a center of community activity" (Queen Creek 2005).

Unlike the cities above, Plainfield, Illinois, requires three amenities. Their code states that the developer "shall incorporate a public space, such as a plaza, courtyard or landscape garden within the vicinity of the structure's main pedestrian entrance of the development's principle structure and shall incorporate a minimum of three of following: pedestrian seating in the form of benches or ledges, water features, seasonal plantings, textured paving, raised brick planters with landscape, pedestrian-scale lighting, sculpture or other artwork, outdoor eating or a café" (Plainfield 2005).

Community amenities, such as seating areas and art, can add to the aesthetics of a development; they must be placed where they will actually be used, however, to be successful amenities. A fountain with seating in the middle of a parking lot is unlikely to be used. The community amenity

Communities increasingly are asking big-box retailers and shopping center developers to include community amenities as part of the development in order to create a more aesthetically pleasing development and provide spaces for people to interact outside of the store. These amenities vary from fountains to parks to clock towers.

In responses to the survey, we found design standards that require a big-box site to include sidewalks that connect transit stops, parking areas, and public sidewalks.

locations should be carefully evaluated. Deltona Beach, Florida, requires developers to:

> configure new buildings so they complement outdoor spaces of existing buildings; walkways, entrances and gathering areas should have shading features, such as trees, landscaping, trellis structures, projecting canopies, covered walkways, arcades, porticos, building orientation etc; located seating areas and benches in shaded areas that are close to activity but that will not block or cause congestion in circulation or at entrances; seating that is built in to low walls is encouraged; outdoor public drinking fountains are encouraged and should be in shaded areas but in circulation routes; public open space should be close to activity and primary circulation and entrances; they should be generally located in larger, more prominent easily accessed areas; courtyards are encouraged and separated from general circulation and are enhanced by detailing and landscaping; outdoor employee area should integrated into site design and should be separated from general public circulation with screening and should have lighting and shading that is adequate. (Deltona Beach 2004)

Beyond the community amenities described above, two cities also require public art as part of the big-box development. Queen Creek requires all big-box retail install public art visible by pedestrians and "reflective of the agrarian heritage of Queen Creek" (Queen Creek 2005). Deltona Beach, Florida, also requires public art but defines art broadly to include "water features, walls, benches, bridges, paving, gates, bike racks, kiosks and other nontraditional art" (Deltona Beach 2005).

Before requiring community amenities, planners should determine what amenities people really want and where they will be most effective. If every developer of a big-box retail establishment were, for example, to choose a clock tower to satisfy the amenity requirement, the community ends up with a series of big boxes all marked by clock towers. Amenities are a good idea, but communities need to be careful not to give the developer too much carte blanche in determining the nature of the specific amenity for the specific development.

Pedestrian and Bicycle Access

Big-box retailers are largely automobile oriented. There has been limited attention to pedestrian and bicycle access to big-box sites. But this is changing. Access for pedestrians, cyclists, and transit riders may be especially important in infill areas (e.g., urban stores) or in inner-city areas where customers are less likely to have access to a car.

In responses to the survey, we found design standards that require a big-box site to include sidewalks that connect transit stops, parking areas, and public sidewalks. Most of the cities require the sidewalks to be buffered by landscaping. And most require raised or different materials for crosswalks. Several cities require sidewalks in big-box sites that are wider than those required for other uses:

- Chandler, Arizona: 6 feet
- Queen Creek, Arizona: 8 feet
- Tucson, Arizona: 8 feet
- Toledo, Ohio: 6 feet
- Bend, Oregon: 5 feet

Queen Creek and Tucson, Arizona, require sidewalks have a landscape strip for their entire length, and sidewalks must have shading on the sidewalk during the major part of the day (Queen Creek 2005; Tucson 2005).

Deltona, Florida, requires bike facilities, including wide travel lanes, striped bike lanes, off-road pathways, and bike-parking facilities, on big-box sites. Bike parking is required close to the building entrance and should be clearly visible. The city prefers bicycle parking areas that are covered, providing shade and protection from rain. The city specifies that U-shaped loop racks or similar design instead of ribbon or wave-type racks, which are less effective for locking the bike (Deltona 2004).

Moline, Illinois, requires big-box developers to create connections to existing and planned pedestrian/bicycle facilities in the community and in surrounding neighborhoods. The developer must provide secure bicycle parking areas (Moline 2005).

In order to encourage greater pedestrian and bicycle activity, each major retail site should include internal circulation routes so that people can conveniently and safely access the store. This means having clearly marked pedestrian paths through the parking lot and to the building. Additionally, there should be a connection between city sidewalks and internal pedestrian circulation for the development.

Green Design

Austin, Texas, has proposed commercial design standards that will include an incentive to have large-scale retailers construct buildings that meet Austin's Green Building program requirements (Katie Larsen, e-mail correspondence with author, July 19, 2005). Currently buildings constructed in the downtown must earn a "one-star green building rating," based on a 2003 ordinance. LEED has several levels of rating including certified, silver, gold, and platinum. To be certified, a building must receive at least 26 points: 33 points gives it a "silver" designation; 39 points gives it a "gold" designation; and 52 points means it's a "platinum" development. The city believes that big-box retailers will agree to the new standards "to reach the city's affluent student and high-tech base" (Kirk 2005).

Green design standards offer an opportunity for cities to enhance the environmental sustainability of their community. As reported in the trends section of this report, retailers are starting to take notice of the benefits of green design and are incorporating green design principles into their buildings. Chicago has been successful in getting Target to produce four LEED-certified buildings in the city. The use of development incentives for the construction of LEED-certified buildings is one method that may prove effective for reducing the environmental impact of big-box retailers.

Traffic Impact Studies

As would be true for any large-scale, auto-oriented development, big-boxes cause traffic problems. Tucson, Arizona, takes an approach to regulating big-box traffic that goes beyond the typical traffic impact analysis. The developer must have a professional entity perform a traffic impact analysis (Tucson 2005). The report must have the scope and criteria for the analysis approved by the city's department of transportation prior to submittal. The report must identify traffic flow impacts on public streets, recommend mitigation measures to address conditions falling below standards set by the city's Mobility Management Plan, and show how the applicant will make recommended improvements.

Moline, Illinois, requires a traffic impact analysis performed by the applicant's traffic engineer. The development must not adversely impact off-site public roads, intersections, and interchanges during the traffic peak associated with a full parking lot. Where the project adversely affects off-site traffic, the city may deny the development application, require a size reduction in the proposed development, or require off-site improvements (Moline 2005).

The use of development incentives for the construction of LEED-certified buildings is one method that may prove effective for reducing the environmental impact of big-box retailers.

The justification for using economic impact analyses as a means of deciding whether to permit big-box development is analogous to the justification for environmental impact assessments.

Economic Impact Analysis

As noted at the outset of this report, there has been a gradual evolution of regulations that apply to big-box retailers. Design, while still a deservedly major focal point of regulation, is giving way to wider concerns that planners cannot effectively address with traditional land-use regulation. Innovative approaches (e.g., formula business ordinances) attempt to give cities a triggering device for deeper review of the impacts of certain types of businesses. Economic impact statements appear to be the cornerstone of community efforts when the concern is that big-box retail practices may have detrimental effects on local wages and business. The justification for using economic impact analyses as a means of deciding whether to permit big-box development is analogous to the justification for environmental impact assessments. As noted by Boarnet et al. (2005):

> [L]and use controls initially prohibited undesirable activities altogether, but later came to permit them in some instances but not others, and later still to mitigate the negative impacts of otherwise desirable activities. If the regulation of superstores [the focus of the Boarnet article] evolves in similar fashion, planners would need to first credibly document the scale, scope, and distribution of impacts. If community costs exceed benefits, the project could be rejected. Or, if benefits exceeded costs but their distribution was objectionable, the project could be rejected (and substantial benefits foregone) or approved with modifications to mitigate its costs. The last has the most appeal, as it captures the benefits while explicitly addressing objections.

These analyses can be expensive and require significant administrative staff time for evaluation and review. A community needs to determine if existing staff is capable and able to review these documents. The California legislature passed a bill in 2004 to make the retailer responsible for paying for the impact assessment, but the governor vetoed the bill.

Oakdale, California, requires all major retail developments to prepare an economic study including a market analysis determining the trade area of proposed development, the present and future population within the trade area, data on effective buying power within the trade area, the projected number of jobs created by the development, estimated wages, and estimated tax revenue (including estimates of shifts from existing similar retailers and projected sales figures for the development) (Oakdale n.d.).

Greenfield, Massachusetts, requires an economic impact assessment as part of its special permit process for projects larger than 20,000 square feet or those that generate more than 500 vehicle trips per day. Approval of the special permit is contingent upon the developer demonstrating that the project will not lead to a net decline in employment or tax revenue, or undermine the downtown business district. Additionally, approval depends on the finding that the project will not unduly burden the provision of public services and infrastructure. (Greenfield 1991).

The latter cost is a significant consideration, as demonstrated in a study commissioned by the Town of Barnstable, Massachusetts. The study, conducted by Tischler and Associates (2002), found that per thousand square feet of development, big-box retail generated an average local revenue of $554 and a cost of $1,023. This generated an annual deficit of $468 per thousand square feet as compared with a deficit of $314 for traditional shopping centers and a surplus of $326 for "specialty retail."

Similarly, Delaware, Ohio, requires a Community Impact Assessment (CIA) for commercial projects on sites larger than one acre or larger in size than 20,000 square feet. In addition to other areas of review, the assessment covers:

- adjacent land uses;

- impact on public services in the form of tax revenue generated;

- police and fire needs;

- traffic generation;

- any intention to request financial incentives (e.g. tax abatement, tax increment financing) and the intended amount; and

- the project's short- and long-term economic impact (specifically: "the need for both this type of project and for additional private or public supporting facilities that may arise as a result of the proposed development") at local, county, and regional levels.

An impact assessment is not required for any property for which one has been conducted in the last six months. (Delaware 2001).

In 2004, Los Angeles adopted an ordinance requiring an economic impact assessment for any proposed retail store larger than 100,000 square feet and with more than 10 percent devoted to nontaxable merchandise (in California, this includes groceries). The ordinance applies in the city's enterprise, empowerment, renewal community zones, community redevelopment agency project areas, and earthquake project areas and to the area extending one mile outside the boundaries of those areas.

The economic impact report must consider all of the following criteria:

Efforts to establish a market larger than 20,000 square feet within the Impact Area have been unsuccessful or whether the proposed use will have an adverse impact or economic benefit on grocery or retail shopping centers in the Impact Area;

The Superstore would result in the physical displacement of any businesses, and, if so, whether the nature of the displaced businesses or would create economic stimulation in the Impact Area;

The Superstore would require the demolition of housing, or any other action or change that results in a decrease of extremely low, very low, low or moderate income housing on site;

The Superstore would result in the destruction or demolition of any park or other green space, playground, childcare facility, or community center;

The Superstore would provide lower in cost and/or higher in quality goods and services to residents than currently available or that are currently unavailable from a cost benefit perspective within the Impact Area in which the project is proposed to be located;

The Superstore would displace jobs within the Impact Area or provide economic revitalization and/or job creation. For purposes of determining this impact, the applicant must identify the number of jobs displaced or created, the quality of the jobs, whether the jobs are temporary or permanent, and the employment sector in which the lost jobs are located;

The Superstore would have a fiscal impact either positive or negative on City tax revenue;

Any restrictions exist on the subsequent use of the property on which the Superstore is proposed to be located, including the provisions of a lease if applicable, which, in the event the owner or operator of the Superstore vacates the premises, would require the premises to remain vacant for a significant amount of time;

The Superstore will result in any materially adverse or positive economic impacts or blight on the Impact Area; and

Any measures are available which will mitigate any materially adverse economic impacts, if any, identified by the applicant, if necessary.

The purpose of the ordinance was to focus on the impacts of a big-box store in economically distressed or redeveloping areas (Los Angeles 2004).

Vallejo, California, requires that the city and developer "shall analyze the short- and long-term economic impacts of the proposed development and shall at a minimum include the following in the analysis":

- a survey of existing stores that provide retail sales and food and beverage sales within the retail, food and beverage market areas that would be served by the proposed superstore, regardless of whether such stores are within the political boundaries of the city and that are likely to be economically affected by the proposed superstore, including the current average retail sales of each store identified therein;

- the geographic vicinity of the stores identified in this survey shall comprise a geographic area referred to as Affected Area;

- a survey of the existing, proposed and/or pending superstores within the Affected Area, a survey of the number of persons who are employed on either full time or a less than full time basis by the existing stores described in Section 16.76.040(C)(1) and (2) above and an estimate of the number of persons who would be employed on both a full time or a less than full time basis by the proposed store;

- the short- and long-term effect proposed superstore could have on the retail stores specified in Section 16.76.040(C)(1) and (2) above, which shall include an analysis of the proposed superstore's potential impact on the following within the Affected Area: retail sales, food and beverage sales, store closures, jobs, property values of other retail sales and food and beverage stores and any food and beverage and/or retail stores that could potentially close, including an analysis of the potential for using the closed site(s) for similar or other uses and such analysis shall consider population trends in the Affected Area, as identified through census bureau data, building permits and other regional trend info;

- both the short- and long-term potential effects of the proposed superstore on retail and food and beverage sales in the Affected Area, including a conclusion as to whether the proposed superstore would cause a net increase or decrease in retail and food and beverage sales in the Affected Area;

- a fiscal impact analysis including but not limited to an analysis of the projected sales tax revenues for the proposed superstore and an analysis of both the short and long term effects of the proposed superstore on net sales tax revenues generated by existing retail and food and beverage stores in the City;

- [an explanation of] the factors used in conducting the analysis and shall also analyze the fiscal impacts, if any, that the proposed superstore would have on City services, including police and fire services and traffic and traffic-related maintenance, to the extent that such impacts are not addressed in a document prepared pursuant to the California Environmental Quality Act;

- where applicable, both the affected store and any other tenants in the affected retail center(s);

- the proposed superstore's potential short and long term net effect on the ability of consumers in the Affected Area to obtain a variety of food and beverage and retail products in light of the analysis conducted pursuant to Section 16.70.040(C)(4) concerning potential closure of retail and/or food and beverage stores within the Affected Area

- a survey of the wage and benefits differentials, if any, between the proposed superstore and existing retail and food and beverage stores in the Affected Area.

- the average savings a typical consumer might enjoy, if any, by the approval of the proposed superstore;

- to be considered by the Planning Commission and City Council (when appropriate) at time of consideration of conditional use permit. (Vallejo n.d.)

Other local efforts at economic impact review, including those for Carbondale, Colorado; Homer, Alaska; Middletown, Rhode Island; Mt. Shasta, California; and Santa Cruz, California, are documented at www.newrules.org/retail/impact.html.

Economic impact assessments, like environmental impact assessments, offer the ability to match regulatory intervention to a demonstrated negative outcome resulting from approval of this type of development.

Wage and Benefit Standards

Big-box retailers can bring a large number of jobs to a community, but these jobs are generally low-wage and provide little in the way of benefits. Some cities in the United States are regulating businesses based on the adequacy of the health care benefits they provide to employees. Wage and benefits ordinances are typically out of the scope of how planners regulate big-box retail. We include them here, however, as part of our comprehensive analysis of regulatory strategies that address one of the "problems" presented by big-box retail.

In July, 2005 the City of New York passed legislation that requires all large food retailers to offer a minimum level of health care benefits. The legislation covers grocery stores with a minimum of 35 employees or other retailers that use 10,000 square feet or more to sell grocery items.

According to council member Christine Quinn "one goal was to create a barrier that would keep Wal-Mart out of the city unless it increased health benefits to workers" (Lieberman 2005). The New York University School of Law helped draft the legislation following a study that critiqued Wal-Mart's health benefits. Some of their criticisms include the six-month waiting period before full-time employees can qualify for coverage and the two-year waiting period for part-time employees to qualify for coverage. The study found that it can cost up to $3 per hour to pay for health benefits, and when employees make less than $20,000 per year, health coverage can become unaffordable. The city decided that grocers are a good place to start (Lieberman 2005).

Wal-Mart contends that the ordinance is discriminatory towards discount-seeking customers. They argue that customers will now have to travel to New Jersey to shop at Wal-Mart. That will not stop Wal-Mart from looking for potential locations within New York City (Lieberman 2005).

In 2005, Maryland passed a bill requiring organizations with 10,000 employees or more in that state to spend at least 8 percent of their payroll on health benefits or place the money directly into the state's health program for the poor (Wagner and Barbaro 2005).

WHAT TO DO WHEN THE BIG BOX CLOSES: "WHITE ELEPHANT" ORDINANCES AND ADAPTIVE REUSE

When big-box retailers close, the remaining vacant sites can pose major problems to communities because these buildings, designed to serve a specific purpose, are often hard to fill with other uses. According to the *Washington Post*, in 2004 Wal-Mart alone had more than 245 vacant buildings nationwide (Stringer 2004). Cities have responded to this problem through programs that help ensure the money is there to demolish buildings, redevelop sites, or find new tenants.

White Elephant Ordinances

In 2005, Wauwatosa, Wisconsin, put in place a requirement that big-box retailers set aside money for demolition should one of their buildings be abandoned. Nancy Welch, Community Development Director, stated the ordinance is intended to protect the city from the vacant boxes scattered

When big-box retailers close, the remaining vacant sites can pose major problems to communities because these buildings, designed to serve a specific purpose, are often hard to fill with other uses.

throughout the country (Johnson 2005). Business groups in the community did not want to use demolition bonds for this purpose (Nancy Welch, e-mail correspondence with author, June 28, 2005). After staff worked with the development community, the ordinance was modified to require that a developer planning a project with 50,000 or more square feet of retail to place money in the city's Land Conservation Fund prior to the issuance of a building permit. The fee is $0.20 per square feet of retail space. A fixed cost was strongly supported by the development community because "it represented a specific amount that could be included in the development costs for the site" (Welch 2005). The property owner or operator, within 12 months of closure, must submit a plan for the removal or reuse of the facility. If the owner/operator fails to provide a plan, the city's Land Conservation Fund is tapped to ensure appropriate redevelopment or reuse of the facility (Wauwatosa 2005).

Oakdale, California, requires an abandoned building surety bond. The ordinance states the property owner:

> shall obtain, provide evidence to the City and carry in full force and effect throughout the duration of the life of the project, or time period as may be stipulated by a development agreement, a performance/surety bond providing for demolition of the primary building or buildings as identified by City; said performance/surety bond shall provide funds to cover the cost of complete building demolition and maintenance of the vacant building site if the primary building is ever vacated or abandoned and remains vacant or abandoned for a period of more than 12 consecutive months following primary business closure. (Oakdale 2005)

Cities sometimes must deal with big-box retailers that use their leases to limit a landlord's ability to release the property for big-box retail or other uses. Forsyth County, Georgia, combats this problem by prohibiting individual retail establishments larger than 75,000 square feet from entering into a lease agreement that precludes the landlord from marketing and renting to future lessees once a tenant has vacated the premises (Forsyth County 2005). If such a store becomes vacant, the property owner is responsible for leasing or selling the property within 24 months. If a lease/sale or pending lease/sale does not occur within 24 months, the county reserves the right to develop plans for the removal or adaptive reuse of the principal structure. Additionally, the property owner is required to provide security patrols to deter vandalism and other illegal activities in and around the vacant structure.

Adaptive Reuse

The reuse of big-box buildings for other purposes can be difficult. These spaces are huge and, as one of the cases below indicate, can be expensive to adapt for other purposes. Furthermore, as Ron Kitchens, President of the Corpus Christi, Texas, Regional Economic Development Authority, noted, "If the buildings didn't work for the biggest retailer, then they're probably not going to work for other retailers. . . . Communities have to be creative" (Stringer 2004). Nevertheless, there have been success stories, as we discuss below. Cities should try to put into place some partnership with the big-box retailer (or make it mandatory) to help the city fill empty big-box stores. Some of the retailers already do this, either with the city or private sector partners, as in the case of attracting call center tenants, which have proven to be apt uses for abandoned big-box buildings.

In 1998, MCI Telecommunications opened a new call center in a former Wal-Mart store in Winchester, Kentucky. The call center provides technical support and help desk functions for hardware and software companies. MCI is the outsourcing operator and provides services for other companies. MCI created a total of 500 jobs when the call center opened.

Big-box stores are easy to convert for call center use. The ability to reuse a big-box store for a call center is driven by the availability of labor. Most of the call centers are for inbound purposes, which require a higher skill set. Call centers typically cost $25 to $40 per square foot for tenant improvements and include the addition of UPC panels and generators, according to Larry Patrick, Manager of Economic Development for Wal-Mart Realty. Wal-Mart works with national firms in identifying call center locations. Firms such as Price Waterhouse obtain basic labor information and then work with Wal-Mart to identify available buildings on a national basis.

When Wal-Mart knows they are planning to close a store, the company's stated practice is to notify the mayor and economic development officials in the community approximately two years in advance. When the city identifies a future tenant, Wal-Mart works with local and state economic development officials to put together an incentive package (Patrick 2004).

When Wal-Mart planned to close its store in the Mobile, Alabama, area, for example, it worked with the Mobile Area Chamber of Commerce economic development staff. Through working together they were able to identify an ideal replacement. The St. Francis-Thomas Medical Center was looking for a flexible space with plenty of parking. The medical center transformed an 81,000- square-foot Wal-Mart store into a center for outpatient services, radiation therapy, and other medical uses. This type of conversion was expensive: renovation costs were approximately $100 per square foot, according to Larry Patrick with Wal-Mart Realty.

Figure 47. *This MCI call center in Winchester, Kentucky, was once a Wal-Mart.*

Figure 48. *The Thomas Medical Center in Daphne, Alabama, was once a 180,000-square-foot Wal-Mart.*

Figure 49.
Miami,
Oklahoma, found
a way to convert
a Wal-Mart to
a community
church.

Wal-Mart Realty

Wal-Mart Realty has personnel that focus specifically on the selling and leasing of empty stores for other purposes. Since 1993, Wal-Mart Realty has converted more than 7.5 million square feet of store space to new uses. In 2004, the company converted 12 stores to new uses (see Table 4).

TABLE 4. ADAPTIVE REUSE OF WAL-MART STORES DURING 2004

New Use	Location	Lease/Sale	Size (square feet)
First Christian Church	Keokuk, IA	Sale	91,500
Wal-Mart Jewelry Repair	Marlow, OK	Wal-Mart Reuse	34,875
Jostens Jewelry Warehouse	Shelbyville, TN	Lease	72,413
Mercedes Benz Dealership	Fife, WA	Sublease	35,360
Randall County Offices	Canyon, TX	Sale	50,968
Health Care Services	Huntington, WV	Sale	129,823
South Central Regional Medical Center	Laurel, MS	Sale	105,583
Topway Enterprises	Houston, TX	Sale	129,391
Incredible Pizza—Entertainment	Warr Acres, OK	Lease	52,200
Maico Theaters	Jacksonville, AR	Lease	40,000
The Gym	Georgetown, KY	Lease	20,509
First Tennessee Bank Call Center	Knoxville, TN	Lease	80,000
Lason—Call Center	Newman, GA	Lease	27,236
White Chevrolet Automobile Dealership	Roanoke Rapids, NC	Lease	89,944
Aldretti Speedway	Alpharetta, GA	Lease	97,912
Dream City—Community Center	Holy Springs, MS	Sale	47,246
Autohaus Automobile Dealership	Lexington, NE	Sale	85,899
Genz–Ryan Pumbing and Heating–Warehouse/Office/Storage	Burnsville, MN	Not Available	104,021

Source: Wal-Mart Realty

In Austin, Minnesota, K-Mart closed a 77,000-square-foot store. At first, the community found it difficult to attract another retailer to reuse the space. However, the once-vacant store is now home to Hormel Foods Corporation's 60,500-square-foot headquarters and a 16,500-square-foot Spam Museum. Hormel decided to locate in the former K-Mart because it was close to its existing corporate offices, had Interstate highway access, and abundant parking. Hormel's investment transformed an unattractive empty big-box into an attractive and popular destination for the community and tourists.

In Prince William County, Virginia, four big-box retailers closed. Hechinger, a former nursery with 108,000 square feet, sat vacant for seven years, becoming a dumping ground for trash. According to Donald Hopper, CFO with Cowles Ford, the dealership purchased the 13.7-acre site in 2003. Cowles decided to spend $5 million to make improvements to the site in order to convert the building for use as a service facility and car wash (Donald Hopper, e-mail correspondence with author, 2005). In addition, the building is being used for a display area for vehicles. The project was completed in the fall of 2004 and has brought the property back to a productive use.

Big-boxes can be reused by other retailers. There are several retailers nationally that locate many of their stores in empty big-box locations. These retailers are able to save costs on rent, while the community benefits from a new retailer. Craft stores such as Jo-Ann Fabrics and Hobby Lobby have used this strategy. Other examples of firms locating in empty big-boxes include discount retailers, such as Burlington Coat Factory and Big Lots.

Figure 50. The Hormel Company in Austin, Minnesota, converted a Wal-Mart into corporate offices and a museum.

In New Orleans, after a Wal-Mart store closed in the Terrytown area, investors saw this as a ripe opportunity to provide a commercial center for the 25,000 people in the area from eastern Asia. The 140,000-square-foot store was transformed into the Hong Kong Plaza and includes food markets, restaurants, beauty salons, jewelry stores, and a tea house (Roberts 2005). The developer Hai Duong believes the plaza will be used as a cultural center for the Asian community. Before the opening of this center, Asians frequently drove to Houston to obtain Asian goods.

Other Regulatory Approaches

Tax sharing. It is not uncommon for cities to fight over who gets the big-box retailer because of competition for tax revenue. This can especially be the case in cities that rely heavily on sales tax revenue. Some cities are now realizing the benefits of developing tax-sharing agreements for big-box development.

In Texas, the cities of Arlington and Kennedale developed an intergovernmental agreement to share tax revenues from a proposed Wal-Mart store. The

Some cities are now realizing the benefits of developing tax-sharing agreements for big-box development.

store will be built in southwest Arlington, with the parking lot being located in Kennedale. Both cities will participate in developing road improvements around the proposed store. The 211,010-square-foot Wal-Mart store will be on a 26-acre wooded site. The site also includes three pad sites for restaurants and retailers. In 2004, the cities entered into an interlocal agreement so that Kennedale receives 25 percent of the sale tax revenues and Arlington would be responsible for providing police and fire service to the store and parking lot. Under this agreement, Kennedale expects to receive $200,000 in sales tax revenue each year from the project (Caldwallader 2005).

The state of California passed Proposition 11, which amended the state constitution to allow cities and counties to enter into sales-tax-sharing agreements. Other states have similar legislation enabling cities to enter into tax-sharing agreements. This tool allows for regional thinking about the retail tax base and can aid in eliminating the fight over big-box retailers.

State initiatives. Several states have proposed legislation to place some control over big-box retailers. The approaches vary from taxation, intergovernmental review, and prohibition of big-boxes. Only one state, Vermont, has successfully passed legislation to date. For an excellent overview of the big-box challenge in Vermont, see *The Vermont Journal of Environmental Law*, Volume 6, 2004–2005, which contains the papers from a symposium held in 2005. The volume is available online at www.vjel.org/index.php.

In 1970, Vermont passed Act 250, which requires all developments of regional impact to obtain a land-use permit from the state's environmental commissions. The act applies to commercial developments that have 10 or more acres. Approval is contingent on the environmental and economic impacts. The act has limited the number of big-box retailers in the state. Wal-Mart has four stores in Vermont, but three of the four, which range in size from 52,000 to 75,000 square feet, are smaller than Wal-Mart's typical store. The Rutland store is located in the city's downtown and replaced a vacant K-Mart (New Rules 2005).

Three states have proposed bills that would tax the revenue of big-box retail stores:

- Minnesota has proposed a tax on retail stores that have more than $20 million annually in sales and either do not have employee compensation greater than $22,000 per year or have more than one-quarter of the employees working less than full-time (Institute for Local Self Reliance 2005c). The proposal, as of March 2006, was still in committee.

- The Maine bill proposes a 3 percent tax on the total sales of any stores larger than 60,000 square feet located outside of a downtown. Two-thirds of the revenue generated from the tax would be used to support a state health care program, and one-third would be used by the State's Small Enterprise Growth Fund (Institute for Local Self Reliance 2005b). The proposal died in the House.

- Montana has proposed a bill to tax big-boxes that generate more than $20 million in sales. The bill applies to those retailers where more than one-quarter of the employees work less than full time and earn wages of less than $22,000 per year. The tax is imposed on a sliding scale based on total store sales. For stores generating between $20 million and $30 million, the tax rate would be 1 percent; between $30 million and $40 million, the tax rate would be 2 percent; and for stores with sales greater than $40 million, the tax rate would be 2 percent. A typical Wal-Mart store generates $70 million in sales per year. The state estimates that the tax would generate $15 million in 2006 (Institute for Local Self Reliance 2005a). Supporters of the bill cited recent studies showing many children of Wal-Mart employees are enrolled in low-income health care programs, saying such stores may make their money off neglecting workers but ultimately cost society more in government assistance (Billings Gazette 2005). The bill was ultimately tabled in committee.

In 2005, the New Jersey Senate proposed a bill to define "superstore retailer." The bill would have allowed municipalities adjacent to a proposed big-box store to have a say in the development approval process. An intermunicipal impact advisory board within the State Department of Community Affairs would have overseen the approval process (Dressel 2004). Even though the proposed bill did not pass, one outcome was positive for New Jersey workers: all Wal-Mart's built in New Jersey in the next five years must use union contractors and union builders (New Jersey Contractors Association 2005).

In 2004, a California bill that would require big-box retailers to pay for the costs of an economic impact report also required that big-box retailers not abandon towns. The bill was proposed as a result of a study by the Bay Area Economic Forum (Ryan 2004). The bill passed both houses but was vetoed by the governor.

RECOMMENDATIONS

Cities need to recognize the importance of addressing big-box retail uses in the planning process for a number of reasons—most importantly the fact that consumers clearly want them and the retailers themselves are determined to find their way into new markets. Most planning offices have little understanding of how large retailers work or how they influence the development of the city and region. By incorporating large retail into the comprehensive plan, probably most appropriately in the economic development element, cities will have a better understanding of the transportation and neighborhood effects of large-scale retailers. Such inclusion will require that planners think through the issues we have presented in this report. The plan will also provide a basis that will help protect any regulations the locality develops from legal challenge.

A similar regional study of retail is also appropriate. Regional competition for tax generators makes this even more important than a local study. By not allowing the retailer to play one municipality off against others in the region, localities can dispense with incentives to these retailers if it is shown that the windfall of one community is a wipeout in others. Furthermore, determining the best location for a big-box retailer in a region can help a variety of communities in seeking a balance between large and small, nationally owned and locally owned businesses. Planners can easily develop an inventory of regional big-box retailers through these retailers' websites. Most have a store locator that would allow a planner to determine the location of all stores in the region.

Using a GIS system, planners can map the location of existing big-box stores. Once a city knows where big-box retailers are likely to locate, it can begin to assess how to balance growth in big-box retail with surrounding land uses and infrastructure.

Current and future demand for big-box retail can also be assessed. Areas where big-box retailers are likely to want to locate should be identified. Siting of big-box retail should be guided by a number of questions:

- What are the potential impacts of new retail development on the existing community as well as the larger area? What are the impacts of retail in adjacent communities on your community? *This report strongly supports the use of an economic development impact assessment as a first step in determining whether a community or region should accept a big-box*

This report strongly supports the use of an economic development impact assessment as a first step in determining whether a community or region should accept a big-box retailer; consult the economic development impact assessment methods mentioned in this report to provide a template for your community's efforts.

retailer; consult the economic development impact assessment methods mentioned in this report to provide a template for your community's efforts.

- Once you have the results of an economic impact assessment, do its results conform to the economic development goals of the community and their implementation as expressed in the economic development element of the comprehensive plan? If there is no such element or plan, how has the community derived its goals?

- Does the city currently provide economic development incentives to retailers? Do the results of the assessment indicate that such incentives are a good thing or even necessary?

- What locations in the community are targeted for economic development? Should these areas include a retail component? What incentives would be appropriate, if any, to encourage retail development and what type of retail development?

- How much land is currently used as retail, both in acres and square footage? How does this compare to other cities in your region? How much land is currently zoned for future retail use? Is the city over- or under-zoned for retail? Does the amount and type of retail development conform to the community's vision of its future?

- Where are retailers, particularly big-box retailers, locating and why? Have your plan and regulations been adequate to shape this development in the way the community wants? Is an audit of your plan and regulations in order if the development is not in conformance? Is a moratorium in order?

- What are the demographics of the retail nodes in your community? What types of retailers will these demographics attract?

Once your community has determined that it wants a big-box retailer, the questions can turn to issues of design, infrastructure, and other concerns within the purview of local regulations:

- Are there any industrial zones or abandoned industrial facilities that could be used for retail space? Such infill strategies can save money and fill unused land with productive uses.

- Are there areas of the community that are currently underserved by retail? What types of retail do these areas need? Even in light of negative results from an economic impact assessment, if an area is having a hard time attracting local, "small" businesses (e.g., grocery stores), perhaps a big-box retailer is the answer.

- How can existing retail sites be adapted for future use? White elephants are a problem in many communities. Address this problem upfront before it becomes a problem.

- Are the city's current regulatory approaches adequate to address big-box retail? If design is a pressing issue, does the community have a triggering device (e.g., permit applications for construction, rehabilitation, or expansion of an existing use) for design review? Does it have an adequate "catalog" of design alternatives (like the photos in this PAS Report) to show retailers and citizens what is possible and to inform retailers as to what the community wants?

Example Ordinances

This report has highlighted numerous examples of how cities are dealing with big-box retailers. This appendix provides information on five excellent examples of how to deal with big-box development. Below is a description of each document and a link to the ordinance. Due to the length of the documents and availability on the Internet, the text is not included in this report. Planners should review state laws and consult with their municipal attorney before adapting any big-box regulation in their community.

Plano, Texas: Plano 2004 Zoning Ordinance, Article 3.113 Superstores:

> Plano provides specific design standards related to the building façade. See www.planoplanning.org/devrev/ZoningOrdinance/ZO061305.pdf (accessed December 2, 2005).

Queen Creek, Arizona: Queen Creek Zoning Ordinance, Section 6.17:

> Queen Creek's ordinance applies to all retail buildings with more than 25,000 square feet. The ordinance provides a comprehensive treatment to all aspects of site design, including community spaces, pedestrian access, and public art among others. See www.queencreek.org/publications/ordinance/ART6.pdf (accessed December 2, 2005).

Toledo, Ohio: Toledo Municipal Code, Section 1109.03, Large Scale Retail Projects:

> Toledo has design standards for all new retail buildings with more than 50,000 square feet. It requires parking to be distributed around the building, pedestrian connections must be addressed, requires bus stops, and provides for building design standards. See www.atcontrol.ci.toledo.oh.us/images/Toledo percent20Planning percent20and percent20Zoning percent20Code.pdf (accessed December 2, 2005).

Virginia Beach, Virginia: Retail Establishments and Shopping Centers Ordinance and Guidelines:

> This ordinance provides specific information to developers about building design, roofs, materials, colors, entryways, signage, equipment screening, lighting, site layout, parking, pedestrian access, public space, landscaping, and stormwater retention. The document is structured in an extremely user-friendly format. For each section, the ordinance language, definitions, and example pictures and renderings are provided. The pictures illustrate the exact design features the city requires to be included in any big-box development proposal. See www.vbgov.com/dept/planning/vgn_files/RetailGuidelines.pdf (accessed December 2, 2005).

Winston-Salem, North Carolina: UDO-118 Ordinance Amending Chapter B, Zoning Ordinance of the Unified Development Ordinances:

> This ordinance applies to all buildings with more than 75,000 square feet. The city provides a presentation that includes photographic examples of the standards. In addition, the site provides a link to the codified requirements. See www.cityofws.org/planweb/new/whats_new.htm#Lg-scale percent20dvpt (accessed December 2, 2005).

APPENDIX B
List of References

[Readers are strongly encouraged to visit the websites of big-box retailers. These sites frequently include annual reports, real estate, store location, and contact information that can be helpful in working with big-box retailers.]

Anchorage, Alaska, City of. n.d. "Anchorage Municipal Charter, Code and Regulations Title 21." http://library6.municode.com/gateway.dll/AK/alaska/1?f=templates&fn=default.htm&npusername=12717&nppassword=MCC&npac_credentialspresent=true&vid=default (accessed November 18, 2005).

Associated Press. 2005. "Wal-Mart Experiments with 'Green' Store." www.cnn.com/rssclick/2005/TECH/science/07/20/green.walmart.ap/index.html?section=cnn_latest (accessed July 26, 2005).

Augusta, Georgia, City of. 2005. "Comprehensive Zoning Ordinance of Augusta-Richmond County, Georgia." www.augustaga.gov/departments/planning_zoning/docs/pdf/dev/Zoning percent20Ordinance percent20update percent20may percent202005.pdf (accessed November 30, 2005).

AutoCart. 2005. "Introducing AutoCart Drive-Thru Complexes." www.autocart.biz/sub_mall.php (accessed November 18, 2005).

Bangor Daily News. 2005. "Big-Box Opponents File Lawsuit Against Belfast." Bangor Daily News, 16 March. www.bangordailynews.com/news/templates/?a=110492 (accessed November 18, 2005).

Basker, Emek. 2001. "Job Creation or Destruction?: Labor-market Effects of Wal-Mart Expansion." http://economics.missouri.edu/Working_Paper_Series/2002/WP0215_basker.pdf (accessed January 12, 2006).

Beauchesne, R. M. 2004. Decision on Petition for Write of Mandate. Superior Court of Stanislaus County, California. December 7.

Bend, Oregon, City of. 2005. City of Bend Zoning Ordinance No.NS-1178. www.ci.bend.or.us/docs/Chapter_10_10_Zoning_Regulations.pdf (accessed November 30, 2005).

Beaumont, Constance. 1997. Better Models for Superstores: Alternatives to Big Box Sprawl. Washington, D.C.: National Trust for Historic Preservation

Billings Gazette. 2005. "Tax on Big-Box Stores Rejected by Senate." Billings Gazette, 2 April. www.billingsgazette.com/index.php?tl=1&display=rednews/2005/04/02/build/state/62-bigbox-tax.inc (accessed November 18, 2005).

Boarnet, M., R. Crane, D. Chatman, and M. Manville. 2005. "Emerging Planning Challenges in Retail: The Case of Wal-Mart." Journal of the American Planning Association 71(4): 433-49.

Boswell, Brannon. 2003. "Welcome to Power Town." RetailTraffic, 1 January. http://retailtrafficmag.com/development/trends/retail_welcome_power_town/ (accessed November 18, 2005).

Bradley, Donald. 2000. "Wal-Mart's Hypermart to Become Smaller Supercenter." Kansas City Star, 21 May 21. www.kcstar.com/item/pages/printer.pat,local/37747b22.521,.html May 21. (accessed November 18, 2005).

Buckley, Frank, Jamie McShane, and Parija Bhatnagar. 2004. "No Smiles for Wal-Mart in California." CNN, 7 April 7. http://money.cnn.com/2004/04/07/news/fortune500/walmart_inglewood/ (accessed November 30, 2005).

Building Contractors Association of New Jersey. 2005. "Anti Big Box Bill Shelved, for Now." Government Affairs Report BCANJ. January. www.bcanj.com/Jangov2005.pdf (accessed December 2, 2005).

Bula, Frances. "Council Rejects Wal-Mart." The Vancouver Sun. www.canada.com/vancouversun/

Burnsville, Minnesota, City of. 2005. "Heart of the City." www.burnsvilleheartofthecity.com/overview.htm (accessed November 18, 2005).

Cadwallader, Robert. 2005. "Parking Lot Ok'd for Wal-Mart Store." Fort Worth Star Telegram, 29 July 29, page 5B.

Cape Cod Commission. 1989. "An Act Establishing the Cape Cod Commission." www.capecodcommission.org/act.htm (accessed November 18, 2005).

Casto Corporation. "Redevelopment of Graceland Shopping Center Continues." www.castoinfo.com/about/news.php?action=details&prID=18 (accessed November 18, 2005).

Chandler, Arizona, City of. "City of Chandler Unified Development Manual Chapter 35-1902." http://udm.chandleraz.gov/index.php?aid=89 (accessed November 18, 2005).

CNBC. 2004. "The Age of Wal-Mart: Inside America's Most Powerful Company." 10 November.

CNN. 2005. "Wal-Mart Experiments with 'Green' Store." CNN, 21 July 21. www.cnn.com/2005/TECH/science/07/20/green.walmart.ap/index.html?section=cnn latest (accessed November 18, 2005).

_____. 2004. "No Smiles for Wal-Mart in California." CNN Money Magazine. http://money.cnn.com/2004/04/07/news/fortune500/walmart_inglewood/ April 7 (accessed July 12, 2005).

Columbus, Ohio, City of. "High Street: North of Morse RD Planning Overlay." www.columbusinfobase.org/High percent20North percent20of percent20Morse/High percent20north percent20of percent20Morse.pdf (accessed November 30, 2005).

Cooke, Michael. "Council Item Synopsis." Turlock, California. http://ci.turlock.ca.us/pdflink.asp?pdf=documents/communityplanning/walmart/StaffReport.pdf (accessed November 30, 2005).

Davis, Lisa S. "New Orleans Faces Off with Wal-Mart." Preservation Online, March 19, 2004. www.nationaltrust.org/magazine/archives/arch_story/031904p.htm (accessed November 30, 2005).

Delaware, Ohio, City of. Ordinance number 04-42.

Deltona, Florida, City of. Ordinance No.14-2004 General (Interim) Design Policy for Residential and Commercial Center Development.

Dressel, William G. 2004. "Executive Director of the New Jersey State League of Municipalities, to the mayor regarding S-2080/A-3504 Anti Big-box Bill, 1 December 2004." New Jersey State League of Municipalities. December. www.njslom.org/ml120104.html (accessed November 2005).

Duerkson, Christopher. 2005. Presentation at APA/AICP Zoning Workshop, Washington, D.C., 15 September 15.

Dunkley, Bill, Amy Helling, and David S. Sawicki. 2004. "Accessibility versus Scale: Examining the Tradeoffs in Grocery Stores." Journal of Planning Education and Research 23, no. 4: 347-401.

Easton, Maryland, Town of. 1999. "Big-Box Moratorium Information." Town of Easton, 1999. www.town-eastonmd.com/Moratorium/Ordinance.htm (accessed December 2, 2005).

Easton, Maryland, Town of. 1999. Ordinance No. 399. www.town-eastonmd.com/Ordinance%20399.htm (accessed December 2, 2005).

Eller, Donnelle. 2004. "New Wal-Mart will have New Design." Des Moines Register, 31 December 31. http://desmoinesregister.com/apps/pbcs.dll/article?AID=/20041231/NEWS08/412310351/1029/BUSINESS (accessed November 30, 2005).

Federal Way, Washington, City of. 2005. Article 22-752 Federal Way City Code. http://search.mrsc.org/nxt/gateway.dll/fdwymc?f=templates&fn=fdwypage.htm$vid=municodes:FederalWay (accessed November 18, 2005).

Floyd, Nell L. 2005. "Madison Paves Way for Progress, Prosperity." The Clarion-Ledger, 9 June. www.clarionledger.com/apps/pbcs.dll/article?AID=/20050609/BIZ/506090363/1005 (accessed November 30, 2005).

Forsyth County, Georgia. 2005. Unified Development Code, Chapter 12, Articles XI–XII.

Fruth, William. 2003. The Flow of Money and Its Impact on Local Economies. www.naiop.org/governmentaffairs/growth/fruth_report.pdf (accessed November 30, 2005).

Georgetown-Scott County Planning Commission. n.d. "Big-Box Design Standards." www.gscplanning.com/big_box_design_standards.htm (accessed November 30, 2005).

Gereffi, Paul. 2002. "Grocers Fine-Tune Their Strategies to Compete with Superstores." Retailing Today, May. www.icsc.org/srch/sct/sct0502/page99.html (accessed November 30, 2005).

Gerhard, Ulrike, and Barbara Hahn. 2005. "Wal-Mart and Aldi: Two Retail Giants in Germany." GeoJournal 62: 15-26.

Goldberg, David. 2005. "The Incredible Shrinking Box." Michigan Land Use Institute, 11 September. www.mlui.org/growthmanagement/fullarticle.asp?fileid=16919 (accessed November 30, 2005).

Goll, David. 2004. "Unusual Mall Anchor Tenants Change Mix." MSNBC, 12 April 12. http://msnbc.msn.com/id/4723223 (accessed November 30, 2005).

Grant, Lorrie. 2005. "Luxury, Low Price Mix as some Malls Blend Merchants." USA Today, 2 February 2. www.usatoday.com/money/industries/retail/2005-02-02-mall-usat_x.htm (accessed December 2, 2005).

Greeley, Colorado, City of. City of Greeley Development Code Chapter 18. www.ci.greeley.co.us/cog/PageNewsDetails.asp?fkOrgID=49&pkNewsDetailsID=534 (accessed September 4, 2005).

Herrick, Thaddeus. 2005. "Despite Rising Gas Prices, Pumping Profits is Tough." Start-up Journal, 31 May. www.startupjournal.com/runbusiness/survival/20050531-herrick.html (accessed December 2, 2005).

Houston, Dan, Michael Oden, and William Spelman. 2004. Big-box Retail and Austin: An Independent Review. Austin Independent Business Alliance. http://civiceconomics.com/Big_Box_Review_Final.pdf (accessed December 2, 2005).

Howell, Debbie. 2005. "Suddenly city: Chains answer urge to go urban." DSN Retailing Today, 9 May.

Inks, Robert. 2003. "City Council to Vote on 'Big-Box' Ban." The Daily Texan, 23 October 23. www.dailytexanonline.com/media/paper410/news/2003/10/23/StateLocal/City-Council.To.Vote.On.bigBox.Ban-536579.shtml (accessed December 2, 2005).

Institute for Local Self-Reliance. 2005. "Montana Considers Tax on Big-Box Stores." The Hometown Advantage, 8 February. www.newrules.org/retail/news_slug.php?slugid=283 (accessed December 2, 2005).

_____. 2004. "Flagstaff Enacts Big-Box Limits." The Hometown Advantage, 29 September. www.newrules.org/retail/news_archive.php?browseby=slug&slugid=264 (accessed December 2, 2005).

_____. n.d. "Big Box Tax—Maine." The Hometown Advantage. www.newrules.org/retail/bigboxtaxme.html (accessed December 2, 2005).

_____. n.d. "Big Box Tax—Minnesota." The Hometown Advantage. www.newrules.org/retail/bigboxtaxmn.html (accessed December 2, 2005).

_____. n.d. "Vermont's Act 250." The Hometown Advantage. www.newrules.org/retail/vermont.html (accessed December 2, 2005).

Johnson, Annysa. 2005. "Tosa Wants to put a Lid on Big Boxes." Milwaukee Journal Sentinel, 3 January. www.jsonline.com/new/metro/jan05/289861.asp (accessed December 2, 2005).

Jones, Ken, and Michael Doucet. 1999. "The Impact of Big Box Development on Toronto's Retail Structure." Centre for the Study of Commercial Activity. January. www.csca.ryerson.ca/publications/1999-01.html (accessed December 2, 2005).

Kansas City, Missouri, City of. n.d. Code of General Ordinances Section 80-135. www. kcmo.org (accessed November 18, 2005).

Kirk, Patricia L. 2005. "Big Box Battles." The Slatin Report, 29 June 29. www.theslatinreport.com/top_story.jsp?StoryName=0629austin.txt (accessed December 2, 2005).

Kohls. 2005. "Form 10-K Annual Report Kohls." www.sec.gov/Archives/edgar/data/885639/000119312505055302/d10k.htm (accessed December 2, 2005).

Kroger Great Lakes Division. 2004. "Kroger to Introduce its First Marketplace Concept Store in Columbus During 2004-2005." Kroger, 7 June. www.prnewswire.com/cgi-bin/stories.pl?ACCT=104&STORY=/www/story/06-07-2004/0002188926&EDATE= (accessed December 2, 2005).

Lafayette, Louisiana, City of. n.d. "Frequently Asked Questions-Proposed Wal-Mart Supercenter." www.cityoflafayette.com/faq.asp?categoryid=28#111 (accessed November 18, 2005).

Lieberman, Paul. 2005. "Wal-Mart Hard Sell in Big Apple." Los Angeles Times, 21 August 21. www.latimes.com/ (accessed August 25, 2005). (17-198)

Local 6. 2005. "Ohio Wal-Mart Caters to Amish." Local 6 and Internet Broadcasting Systems, Inc., 17 May. www.local6.com/news/4499629/detail.html (accessed December 2, 2005).

Los Angeles, City of. 2003. Options for Regulating the Development of Superstores. Report No. R-3-0585 City Attorney's Office. December.

_____ 2004. Superstores in Economic Assistance Areas, Municipal Code. www.lacity.org/council/cd13/houscommecdev/cd13houscommecdev239629363_05042005.pdf (accessed March 7, 2006).

Mehta, Chirag, Ron Baiman, and Joe Persky. 2004. "The Economic Impact of Wal-Mart: An Assessment of the Wal-Mart Store Proposed for Chicago's West Side." Chicago: UIC Center for Urban Economic Development. March.

Merriam, Dwight. 2005. Presentation at APA/AICP Zoning Workshop, Washington, D.C., 15 September.

Miller, Jessica. 2004. "New Urbanism Projects: The Next Frontier for Big-Box Retailers." National Real Estate Investor, 26 October. http://nreionline.com/news/Big_Box/index.html (accessed December 2, 2005).

Moline, Illinois, City of. Moline Municipal Code Section 35-3419.

Morris, Marya. 2002. "Balancing Trademark Protection with Community Appearance." In Saving Face: How Corporate Franchise Design Can Respect Community Character by Ronald Lee Fleming. Planning Advisory Service Report No. 503/504, pp. 52-53.

Nadel, Barbara A. 1999. "Buying into Green Design." RetailTraffic, 1 September. http://retailtrafficmag.com/mag/retail_buying_green_design/index.html (accessed December 2, 2005).

Nasser, Haya El. 2005. "Mississippi Wal-Marts May Apply 'New Urbanism' in Rebuilding." USA Today. 14 November.

New Jersey Contractors Association. 2005. "Anti Big-box Bill Shelved, For Now." Government Affairs Report BCANJ. www.bcanj.com/Jangov2005.pdf January (accessed July 12, 2005).

NEMO (Nonpoint Education for Municipal Officials). n.d. "Grass Pavers in Overflow Parking Lot." University of Connecticut. http://web.uconn.edu/nemo/case_studies/west_farms_cs.htm (accessed December 2, 2005).

Oakdale, California, City of. n.d. City of Oakdale City Code. http://68.15.49.6/oakdale_ca/lpext.dll?f=templates&fn=site_main-j.htm&2.0 (accessed September 17, 2005; page no longer available)

Paley, Amit R. 2005. "Adjacent Wal-Marts May Dodge Size Curbs." Washington Post, 7 March, B01.

Perry, Theodis L., Jr., and James T. Noonan. 2001. Big-Box Retail Development. Maryland Department of Planning, 2001. www.mdp.state.md.us/mgs/bigbox/bigbox_v3.pdf (accessed December 2, 2005).

Peterson, Rachel. 2005. "Big-box Limits Rejected." Arizona Daily Sun, 18 May.

Plainfield, Illinois, Village of. Village of Plainfield's Site Plan Review Ordinance No.2264.

Plano, Texas, City of. 2004. City of Plano 2004 Zoning Ordinance Article.113. www.planoplanning.org/devrev/ZoningOrdinance/ZO061305.pdf (accessed November 30, 2005).

Powell, Ohio, City of. n.d. Codified Ordinances of Powell, Ohio Section 1147.15 Large Non-Residential Establishments. www.conwaygreene.com/Powell.htm (accessed November 30, 2005).

Queen Creek, Arizona, City of. 1999. Queen Creek Zoning Ordinance Article 6.17, Superstores and Big Box Retail Uses. www.queencreek.org (accessed November 30, 2005).

Quinn, Christopher. 2004. "The World According to Wal-Mart." Atlanta Journal-Constitution, August 22, 2004.

REI. 2004. "REI's New Portland Store Receives United States Green Building Council's LEED Gold Aware for Commercial Interiors." Press release, 11 November 11.

Reidy, J. Michael, and Robert H. McGuckin. 2005. "The Revolution in Retail Trade." Executive Action, no. 142, April. New York, N.Y.: The Conference Board.

Retail Traffic. 2005. "Home Depot and Snacks." RetailTraffic, July 7, 2005. http://retailtrafficmag.com/news/home_depot_snacks/ (accessed December 2, 2005).

_____. 2001. "Municipalities Work to Bridge the Urban Retail Gap." Retail Traffic, 1 April. http://retailtrafficmag.com/mag/retail_municipalities_work_bridge/index.html (accessed December 2, 2005).

RH Johnson Company. 2000. Metropolitan Kansas City: Year 2000 Shopping Center Report, Kansas City, Missouri.

Roberts, Shearon. 2005. "Filling an Empty Big-Box." The Times-Picayune, 28 July. www.nola.com/business/t-p/index.ssf?/base/money-0/112253149779960.xml (accessed December 2, 2005).

Rodino Associates. 2003. Final Report on Research for Big Box Retail/Superstore Ordinance. Prepared for Industrial and Commercial Development Division, City of Los Angeles, Los Angeles, California, October.

Roswell, Georgia, City of. 2004. Roswell Zoning Ordinance Article 3. www.roswellgov.com/Departments.asp?Page=565 (accessed November 30, 2005).

Ryan, David. "Big-Box Bill Comes Too Late for AmCan." 2004. Napa News, 14 September. www.napanews.com/templates/index.cfm?template=story_full&id=8E6315CC-24DA-4E49-8774-738A95F3F738 (accessed July 12, 2005; page no longer available).

San Francisco, City of. n.d. Planning Code Section 703.3. www.sfgov.org/site/planning_index.asp (accessed November 30, 2005).

Santee, California, City of. n.d. "City of Santee Economic Outlook." www.ci.santee.ca.us/dhr/econdev.htm (accessed November 18, 2005)

Santee Trolley Square. n.d. Santee Trolley Square. www.shopsanteetrolleysquare.com/ (accessed December 2, 2005).

Scally, Robert. 2000. "Wal-Mart's New Store in LA to Build on Urban Strategy." Discount Store News, 6 March. www.findarticles.com/p/articles/mi_m3092/is_5_39/ai_60122317?cm_ven=Y&cm_ite=PI (accessed December 2, 2005).

Sembler Company. n.d. Edgewood Retail District. www.sembler.com/synopsis-Sheets/Edgewood percent20Retail.pdf (accessed September 5, 2005; page no longer available).

Sprawlbusters. 2005. "Citizens Win Referendum Vote." Sprawlbusters, 14 June. www.sprawl-busters.com/search.php?readstory=469 (accessed December 2, 2005).

_____. 2005. "State's Supreme Court Gives Voters Right to Referendum on Wal-Mart." Sprawlbusters, 3 July. www.sprawl-busters.com/search.php?readstory=1904 (accessed December 2, 2005).

_____. 2005. "Wal-Mart Superstore Will Go to Voters in November." Sprawlbusters, 1 September. www.sprawl-busters.com/search.php?readstory=1991 (accessed December 2, 2005).

_____. 2004. "Residents Seek to Defeat Big-box Zone Referendum." Sprawlbusters, 24 October. www.sprawl-busters.com/search.php?readstory=1608 (accessed December 2, 2005).

_____. 2004. "Wal-Mart Loses Referendum Due to Anti-Wal-Mart Hysteria." Sprawl-busters, 6 April. www.sprawl-busters.com/search.php?readstory=1793 (accessed December 2, 2005).

Stamford, Connecticut, City of. 2004. Zoning Regulations Section 3. www.cityof-stamford.org/ZoningBoard/PDF/CityOfStamfordZoningRegulations05.pdf (accessed November 30, 2005).

Stone, Kenneth E. 1988. The Effect of Wal-Mart Stores on Businesses in Host Towns and Surrounding Towns in Iowa. Iowa State University, 9 November. www.econ.iastate.edu/faculty/stone/Effect%20of%20Walmart%20-%201988%20paper%20scanned.pdf (accessed December 2, 2005).

Stone, Kenneth, and Georgeanne M. Artz. 2001. "The Impact of 'Big Box' Building Materials Stores on Host Towns and Surrounding Counties in a Midwestern State." Presented at the 2001 AAEA Annual Meeting, Chicago, Illinois, August 5-8. http://amiba.net/pdf/stone_home_improvement_center_study.pdf (accessed January 12, 2006).

Stringer, Kortney. 2004. "Wal-Mart's Surge Leaves Dead Stores Behind." Wall Street Journal, 15 September.

Thalmann, Christopher. 1999. Letter to Easton, Maryland, Planning and Zoning Commission. www.town-eastonmd.com/Moratorium/Thalmann.htm (accessed July 11, 2005)

The Home Depot. 2005. "Form 10-K Annual Report The Home Depot." www.sec.gov/Archives/edgar/data/354950/000104746905009783/a2153171z10-k.htm (accessed December 2, 2005).

_____. 2003. "You've Never Seen a Home Depot Like It!" The Home Depot, 16 April. http://ir.homedepot.com/ReleaseDetail.cfm?ReleaseID=108314 (accessed December 2, 2005).

Thorne, Susan. 2003. "Rising Above the Rest." Shopping Centers Today, October. www.icsc.org/srch/sct/sct1003/page51.php?region= (accessed December 2, 2005).

Tischler & Associates. 2002. Prototype Land Use Fiscal Analysis. Prepared for the Town of Barnstable, Massachusetts

Toledo, Ohio, City of. 2005. Toledo Municipal Code Section 1109.030. www.amlegal.com/nxt/gateway.dll/Ohio/toledo/parteleven-planningandzoningcode/chapter1109designstandards?f=templates$fn=altmain-nf.htm$3.0#JD_Chapter1109.

Tucson, Arizona, City of. 2004. City of Tucson Land Use Code 3.5.9.7. www.tucsonaz.gov/planning/codes/luc/lucweb/Art3div5.html#P1222_84709 (accessed November 18, 2005).

Turlock, California, City of. 2004. Big-box Ordinance. http://ci.turlock.ca.us/citydepartments/communityplanning/bigboxordinance.asp (accessed November 18, 2005).

U.S. Congress. House. Democratic Staff of the Committee on Education and the Workforce. Everyday Low Wages; The Hidden Price We All Pay for Wal-Mart. 2004.

Vallejo, California, City of. n.d. Chapter 16.76 of the Vallejo Municipal Code.

Vancouver, City of. 2005. "Public Hearing Agenda, Tuesday, June 14, 2005." http://vancouver.ca/ctyclerk/cclerk/20050614/ph20050614.htm (accessed November 18, 2005).

_____. 2005. "Notice of Meeting Public Hearing Agenda." http://vancouver.ca/ctyclerk/cclerk/20050628/documents/ph20050614-WM-complete.pdf (accessed November 30, 2005).

Vestar Development Corporation. n.d. Desert Ridge Marketplace. www.vestar.com/ newsite/PropPages/DesertRM.html (accessed December 2, 2005).

Virginia Beach, Virginia, City of. n.d. A User's Guide for City of Virginia Beach Retail Establishments and Shopping Centers Ordinance. www.vbgov.com/dept/planning/vgn_files/RetailGuidelines.pdf (accessed November 30, 2005).

Wagner, John and Michael Barbaro. 2005. "Maryland Rules on Wal-Mart Insurance." Washington Post, 6 April, A01.

Wal-Mart. 2004. "New Orleans, LA 5022." Wal-Mart Facts.Com, 25 August. www.walmartfacts.com/community/article.aspx?id=569 (accessed December 2, 2005).

Wal-Mart. Form 10-K Annual Report Wal-Mart.

www.sec.gov/Archives/edgar/data/104169/000119312505066992/d10k.htm (accessed December 2, 2005).

Wal-Mart. 2005. "Wal-Mart Opens First Experimental Supercenter." Wal-Mart Facts. Com, 20 July. www.walmartfacts.com/newsdesk/article.aspx?id=1241 (accessed December 2, 2005).

Wal-Mart Facts. 2005. "Nationwide Impact." Wal-Mart Facts.Com, 4 November. www.walmartfacts.com/community/nationwide-impact.aspx (accessed December 2, 2005).

Wauwatosa, City of. 2005. Ordinance O-05-45. www.wauwatosa.net/ImageLibrary/Internet/BigBoxOrdinanceFinal.pdf (accessed November 30, 2005).

White, Patrick. 1996. "A Whole Lot of Turf." Turf Magazine, February. Invisible Structures, Inc. www.invisiblestructures.com/GP2/whole_lotof_turf.htm (accessed December 2, 2005).

Winston-Salem, North Carolina, City of. 2005. Unified Development Ordinance 118. www.cityofws.org/planweb/zoningarchive/UDOarchive/udo_2004/udo-118final09202004.pdf (accessed November 18, 2005).

Woods, Walter and Renee DeGross. 2004. "Compact Wal-Mart on Way to Midtown." Atlanta Journal-Constitution, 21 July 21. www.ajc.com/news/content/business/0704/22walmart.html (accessed December 2, 2005).

Making Great Communities Happen

The American Planning Association provides leadership in the development of vital communities by advocating excellence in community planning, promoting education and citizen empowerment, and providing the tools and support necessary to effect positive change.

483/484. Planning for Post-Disaster Recovery and Reconstruction. Jim Schwab, et al. December 1998. 346pp.

485. Traffic Sheds, Rural Highway Capacity, and Growth Management. Lane Kendig with Stephen Tocknell. March 1999. 24pp.

486. Youth Participation in Community Planning. Ramona Mullahey, Yve Susskind, and Barry Checkoway. June 1999. 70pp.

489/490. Aesthetics, Community Character, and the Law. Christopher J. Duerksen and R. Matthew Goebel. December 1999. 154pp.

493. Transportation Impact Fees and Excise Taxes: A Survey of 16 Jurisdictions. Connie Cooper. July 2000. 62pp.

494. Incentive Zoning: Meeting Urban Design and Affordable Housing Objectives. Marya Morris. September 2000. 64pp.

495/496. Everything You Always Wanted To Know About Regulating Sex Businesses. Eric Damian Kelly and Connie Cooper. December 2000. 168pp.

497/498. Parks, Recreation, and Open Spaces: An Agenda for the 21st Century. Alexander Garvin. December 2000. 72pp.

499. Regulating Home-Based Businesses in the Twenty-First Century. Charles Wunder. December 2000. 37pp.

500/501. Lights, Camera, Community Video. Cabot Orton, Keith Spiegel, and Eddie Gale. April 2001. 76pp.

502. Parks and Economic Development. John L. Crompton. November 2001. 74pp.

503/504. Saving Face: How Corporate Franchise Design Can Respect Community Identity (revised edition). Ronald Lee Fleming. February 2002. 118pp.

505. Telecom Hotels: A Planners Guide. Jennifer Evans-Crowley. March 2002. 31pp.

506/507. Old Cities/Green Cities: Communities Transform Unmanaged Land. J. Blaine Bonham, Jr., Gerri Spilka, and Darl Rastorfer. March 2002. 123pp.

508. Performance Guarantees for Government Permit Granting Authorities. Wayne Feiden and Raymond Burby. July 2002. 80pp.

509. Street Vending: A Survey of Ideas and Lessons for Planners. Jennifer Ball. August 2002. 44pp.

510/511. Parking Standards. Edited by Michael Davidson and Fay Dolnick. November 2002. 181pp.

512. Smart Growth Audits. Jerry Weitz and Leora Susan Waldner. November 2002. 56pp.

513/514. Regional Approaches to Affordable Housing. Stuart Meck, Rebecca Retzlaff, and James Schwab. February 2003. 271pp.

515. Planning for Street Connectivity: Getting from Here to There. Susan Handy, Robert G. Paterson, and Kent Butler. May 2003. 95pp.

516. Jobs-Housing Balance. Jerry Weitz. November 2003. 41pp.

517. Community Indicators. Rhonda Phillips. December 2003. 46pp.

518/519. Ecological Riverfront Design. Betsy Otto, Kathleen McCormick, and Michael Leccese. March 2004. 177pp.

520. Urban Containment in the United States. Arthur C. Nelson and Casey J. Dawkins. March 2004. 130pp.

521/522. A Planners Dictionary. Edited by Michael Davidson and Fay Dolnick. April 2004. 460pp.

523/524. Crossroads, Hamlet, Village, Town (revised edition). Randall Arendt. April 2004. 142pp.

525. E-Government. Jennifer Evans–Cowley and Maria Manta Conroy. May 2004. 41pp.

526. Codifying New Urbanism. Congress for the New Urbanism. May 2004. 97pp.

527. Street Graphics and the Law. Daniel Mandelker with Andrew Bertucci and William Ewald. August 2004. 133pp.

528. Too Big, Boring, or Ugly: Planning and Design Tools to Combat Monotony, the Too-big House, and Teardowns. Lane Kendig. December 2004. 103pp.

529/530. Planning for Wildfires. James Schwab and Stuart Meck. February 2005. 126pp.

531. Planning for the Unexpected: Land-Use Development and Risk. Laurie Johnson, Laura Dwelley Samant, and Suzanne Frew. February 2005. 59pp.

532. Parking Cash Out. Donald C. Shoup. March 2005. 119pp.

533/534. Landslide Hazards and Planning. James C. Schwab, Paula L. Gori, and Sanjay Jeer, Project Editors. September 2005. 209pp.

535. The Four Supreme Court Land-Use Decisions of 2005: Separating Fact from Fiction. August 2005. 193pp.

536. Placemaking on a Budget: Improving Small Towns, Neighborhoods, and Downtowns Without Spending a Lot of Money. December 2005. 133pp.

537. Meeting the Big Box Challenge: Planning, Design, and Regulatory Strategies. Jennifer Evans–Crowley. March 2006. 69pp.